SOUL CREW

SOUL CREW

The Inside Story of Britain's Most Notorious Hooligan Gang

David Jones and Tony Rivers

MILO BOOKS

First published in March 2002 by Milo Books

Copyright © 2002 David Jones and Tony Rivers

The moral right of the authors has been asserted.

ISBN 1 903854 08 3

Typeset by Avon DataSet Ltd, Bidford on Avon B50 4JH
Printed and bound in Great Britain by
Creative Print and Design, Ebbw Vale, Gwent

MILO BOOKS
P.O.Box 153
Bury
BL0 9FX
info@milobooks.com

Contents

Foreword   vii

FIRST HALF: DAVE'S STORY
1   Turning Back the Red Army   3
2   A Sea of Diamonds and Bright Colours   12
3   Pass the Dutchie   23
4   New Street Horrors   31
5   The Big One   38
6   The First Picture of Summer   45
7   The Ultimate Season   52
8   Zulu Dawn   67
9   The Famous CFC   73
10   Satellite Wars   80
11   Pump Up The Volume   86

SECOND HALF: TONY'S STORY
12   Small Steps   93
13   The Jacks   105
14   City In Europe   114
15   Court in the Act   124
16   The Road to Wembley   137
17   The Plymouth Brethren   152
18   Yorkshire Men   161
19   Crossing Swords   171
20   Having a Nose   186
21   Bushwhackers   197
22   The Final Whistle   208

Foreword

IN JANUARY 2002, the United Kingdom media was once again full of horror stories about the scourge of football hooliganism. This time the Press had a new bogey team. It was not the Red Army of Manchester United, which had dominated the papers in the 1970s, or the Chelsea Headhunters or Millwall Bushwhackers, the London terrors of the 1980s. Instead it was the followers of a Welsh Second Division side, Cardiff City AFC.

The spark for this torrent of outrage was an FA Cup third-round tie at Ninian Park between Cardiff and Premier League pacesetters Leeds United. Both teams have a reputation for violence among a certain section of their supporters and the game was conducted in a highly-charged atmosphere. Referee Andy D'Urso was pelted with coins and Leeds players were showered with bottles. Fans also invaded the pitch and tried to attack Leeds supporters before being forced back by riot police. Sam Hammam, the Cardiff owner, was accused of inflaming the situation by walking round the pitch in the second half and standing in front of the Leeds contingent. The club was subsequently charged by the Football Association of Wales and Hammam was forbidden from indulging in his customary walkabouts. The police made a series of arrests in the days that followed.

Yet in truth, the episode was relatively trivial to those truly "in the know". There was no fighting: hardly a punch was

thrown in anger all day. The hooligan gangs of Cardiff and
Leeds never clashed, despite a blizzard of pre-match hype.
Little or no damage was done inside or outside the ground.
Hardly anyone was hurt. It could have been far worse.

For the real story is that Cardiff City have, at the moment
we write, perhaps the toughest and most violent soccer gang
in Britain. For 20 years they have gone by the name of the
Soul Crew and for much of that time we were part of that
gang. Members of the Soul Crew would not regard the events
of January 6 as special: indeed, they would dismiss them as a
storm in a teacup. Their mission has been to meet and fight
hooligan gangs of other clubs and, in doing so, to prove their
supremacy. Coin-throwing is not their style.

This is the *real* story of the fighting followers of Cardiff
City: of their formative battles, their victories and (rare)
defeats, of their enemies and allies. It covers three decades of
terrace disorder. It is not intended to encourage anyone to
fight at football matches. Both of us, the authors, have given
that game up. Rather it is an attempt to tell it like it was – and
is – inside a soccer gang.

David Jones and Tony Rivers

FIRST HALF

DAVE'S STORY

CHAPTER ONE

Turning Back the Red Army

IT WAS, wrote one excitable newspaper columnist, the "least long-awaited clash since Boadicea's chariots bumped into the Romans." In the red corner were the most notorious soccer followers of the day: the infamous hordes of the Red Army of Manchester United. In the blue corner were the working class supporters of Cardiff City. The uniform for both sides was a bizarre mix of half-mast "parallel" trousers with three-button waistbands, heavy boots or shoes with enormous heels, feather cuts, scarves tied to wrists, and butcher's coats or crombies. The battleground was Ninian Park.

The match, in September 1974, was described in the book *The Roots of Football Hooliganism* as "a watershed in the reporting of football hooliganism." It was the first time that the clash between the two sets of fans – rather than the game itself – was the main topic of newspaper coverage. Reams of newsprint were devoted to the threat posed by the forthcoming encounter, for in those wild, boot-boy days, the supporters of United stood out above all others for their hooligan reputation. Many wanted to see if the much-vaunted Stretford Enders would finally meet their match among the rugged miners and dockers of South Wales.

I was too young to remember much about that now-infamous match but one of my best mates, Gary, has been following Cardiff for almost 30 years and has probably done every ground in the country. These are his recollections of a game that has passed into hooligan folklore.

I attended my first Cardiff City game when I was fourteen. It was Manchester United at home in the 1974-75 season. What a debut! All the talk amongst the kids in our town that summer was about how the Red Army was going to invade Cardiff and how the Grange End was going to get taken. My 16-year-old brother and his mate Mike, who had already seen a handful of matches the previous season, promised to take me along with them. For the first time in my life I couldn't wait for the six weeks school holidays to end.

We boarded the train at Neath at around 10am and noticed around 20 Swansea fans drinking around the buffet area decked out in skinners/lab coats, tartan, and so on. The Jacks in those days had (and still have) a bad habit of sucking up to other mobs, Chelsea at Ninian Park in 1977 and 1979 being prime examples (even at a recent Cardiff vs. Swansea fixture they have been spotted holding up "Chelsea Headhunters" flags).

As we drew into Port Talbot station, a small group of Cardiff got on: rough-looking bastards in their mid-twenties, probably from the Sand Fields estate, one of the toughest council estates in Europe at the time. Within minutes of the train restarting they were wading into the Swansea lot. One hapless Jack got a full can of Colt 45 in the face. Only when the police got on at Bridgend was order restored.

Whilst exiting Cardiff Central, we passed several Man United at the bottom of the stairs. A few had been badly leathered and one had his head bandaged up like a mummy. Outside around 300 United were held near the bus station with dozens of police dog handlers around them. In those days we didn't really know anybody in Cardiff and we were too young to get into the pubs, so we started to make our way in the direction of the ground. Halfway down Tudor Road, with plenty of time to kill, we stopped off at Del's chippy, a greasy joint with an old coal-fire cooking range. Rumour had it that old Del used to gob into the fat to check it was hot enough. Just as we were leaving the shop we heard a huge chant of, "United, United." With that, around 6-700 Mancs came rampaging up the road, smashing windows and turning cars on their roofs. We dove back into the chippy and one of the customers bolted the door. 'Birch the bloody lot of them,' some old-timer muttered.

Fifteen minutes later, the coast was clear and we carried on towards the ground. My brother's mate seemed worried that we had not seen many Cardiff around and mentioned something about 150 City getting arrested a few days earlier at Bristol City in a League Cup game. On arriving outside the ground, we picked up tickets for the Canton Stand and walked back down to the café opposite Ninian Park station. We stood there with our cans of pop and watched a constant stream of red and white make its way up Sloper Road. Lots were togged up in Bay City Roller gear, others in those zip-up cardigans with horizontal stripes in your team's colours. Wrangler jackets with patches proclaiming "Next to sex, I like United best" also seemed to be the order of the day.

On hearing a large commotion, we looked left under the railway bridge and again a huge crew of United were running up the street, but this time lots of them were looking very worried and none of them were singing. Cardiff were making their way to the ground en masse: 1500-2000, no problem, and the infamous Red Army were on their toes at last. Many kept running straight towards the ground and others ran up the street by the side of the park. I've seen Cardiff turn out some very good mobs over the years, but this was the best, numbers-wise at least.

Taking our seats I remember looking over at the Bob Bank in awe of United's support. There were probably 10,000 Reds there that day. Even before the ground started to fill, we could see hundreds of their boot boys sitting the length of the wall at the back of the terrace. Hundreds more started to assemble at the corner by the Cardiff end, some on the roof of the tea bar throwing stones, or whatever, at the house behind. Others were starting to run at the newly-erected fence that was keeping the two sets of fans apart. From where we were sitting we could see things were getting nasty. Chants of "Aberfan, Aberfan" started to boom from the United lot and a couple of Mancs directly behind us thought it would be a good idea to join in. Cardiff draw a lot of support from the mining communities and villages of South Wales and a lot of people were getting very annoyed around us. Fistfights started breaking out and some of the United lot started asking stewards for transfers onto the terrace.

I went down for a piss just before kick-off and a United fan was lying out cold in the urinal trough. I bet that he hadn't bargained for this down in sheepshagger country. As I got back to my seat the game was underway and Gerry Daly was lining up a third-minute penalty right in front of us. One-nil to United. More scuffles started around the ground and at one point it seemed the whole Grange End charged at the fence in a unit. Police and stewards, some in crash helmets, were trying to battle the mob away at the fence and it appeared Cardiff were trying harder to get at United than they at us. Towards the end of the game Mike commented that he wished we had gone on the Grange End but had secretly thought that United might have massacred Cardiff. How wrong can one be?

We decided to leave the ground five minutes before the final whistle, when the real action would start, and make our way back to the railway station. There was no point in us hanging around: three schoolboys from Neath who probably couldn't have won a fight between us. Walking quickly back down Ninian Park Road we noticed the dozens of windows that had been put through and a few parked cars with their windscreens shattered. Fifty yards ahead we spotted a small mob hanging around on a corner. We didn't have a clue who they were, so we took a detour into one of the side streets, to rejoin the main road further down.

According to the book The Red Army Years, *United wasted Cardiff near the ground and went home happy. Rubbish. We were nearing the station by the Empire Pool when again United came running down the street in panic. Cardiff had steamed in at the crossroads by the old House of Holland furniture store and legged them again. Many people older than me have told me this story and I have no reason to dispute it. Cardiff took United the full distance that day, whatever you hear.*

There was uproar in the local and national press. A very vivid picture on the front page of Monday morning's Daily Mirror *showed a fan being held down and booted in the face. Cardiff City Football Club subsequently tried to introduce ID passes for all under-18s entering the ground in a bid to stamp out the growing hooligan problem. This scheme must have been shortlived as on the launch day, a game with Bristol City, I gained entry by just asking a bloke and his wife if I couldn't tag along with them. For the record Bristol brought a total of 50 travelling fans that day. Not many teams, Villa included, brought large contingents for the remainder of that season.*

It was all too rare for Cardiff City AFC to make the headlines at that time. The club, formed in 1899 as Riverside FC, had joined the Football League in 1920 (along with Leeds United) and in many ways its glory days were over almost before they had begun. In the mid-1920s the club missed out on the League Championship by just 0.024 of a goal as they came second behind Huddersfield: if they had scored a penalty in their final match of the season they would have brought the Championship to Wales. Sadly they missed the penalty. In 1927 they did win the FA Cup but that, in terms of major honours, was that. The next four decades would see the Bluebirds bouncing up and down the divisions until their final (at the time of writing) short stint in the old First Division in the early 1960s. The term sleeping giant has been applied to the club but much of the time they appeared comatose. Like many other teenagers of the time, Gary was finding the antics off the pitch more exciting than the performances on it.

The 1975-76 season saw us playing down in the Third Division. By now I had started to go to a few away games as well as all the home fixtures.

"Fancy going to Millwall away on Saturday?" asked IJ, an old schoolmate of mine.

"Yeah, okay."

We met at Neath station on a cold December morning and brought our £4 half-returns to Paddington. We had something like a fiver left between us to last the day. At the time we must have heard of Millwall's reputation but I don't think we knew the danger we were putting ourselves in. We had no idea how many Cardiff fans would turn up or how many would go by train – just me and IJ, as it turned out. We knew better than to wear colours even in those days but still got sussed out on the train journey down to New Cross Gate. A horrible looking 20-stone sweaty got on at Rotherhithe and sat opposite. He knew straight away that we were Cardiff and asked how many were coming down today. He must have clocked our nervous faces and the fact that we weren't talking to each other. As it turned out he was okay and even walked us down off the Tube, right to the away turnstiles. What would have been the point in him slamming two kids half of his age when he knew there would be plenty of fun on hand later?

We paid into the ground and joined the 300 or so Cardiff behind the goal. For the first time that day we felt reasonably safe and relaxed. We were in amongst some handy-looking Cardiff boys. As the teams came out onto the pitch, a chant of "Come on Millwall" started up and within minutes they started pouring into the away end from the bank on the side of the pitch. Some of the older Cardiff stayed and had a go but most of the others legged it into the far corner where you could get 50p transfers into the side seating. Blokes were fighting to get through and not even bothering to get their change.

At this point I got split up from IJ and had no money to escape into the seats. I was stranded in the away end with the handful of remaining Cardiff fans. We were underneath a floodlight pylon with a couple of police dog handlers trying to hold off Millwall. I remember two mad-bastard brothers from the Rhondda taunting the South Londoners. Somebody told me later they were called the Cole twins.

When police reinforcements finally arrived we were escorted into the seats with all the rest. Even when we thought things couldn't get any worse, Millwall were finding their way in amongst us and by the time the second goal went in they were starting to wade in. More and more Millwall were mobbing up and when goal number three went in Cardiff didn't even bother cheering. The result of the match meant nothing to most us by now; there were far more important things to worry about – like getting out of this shithole alive.

At the final whistle the Old Bill managed to weed out the rest of Millwall who were still with us and then held us outside the ground. They took Cardiff to the coaches and me and IJ discreetly made our way back towards the Tube. We had to walk past a large queue of Millwall waiting to get tickets for a cup tie with Crystal Palace. We could see a bloke handing a Cardiff satin scarf to his son and all his mates laughing: he'd obviously taken it from one of our fans.

But Cardiff would turn the tables when Millwall came for the return match the following April. A mob of 60-70 arrived by train at Cardiff Central at around 1.30pm and police crammed them straight on to a waiting double-decker bus. As they made their way along Tudor Road I remember them barking out threats from the narrow windows of the bus and a bloke with a full-face beard tapping the glass with what looked like a lock knife. Nothing happened before the game as they were taken straight off the bus and into the ground. They had around 150-200 in total.

At the end of the match, Millwall came out and stood in the middle of the road outside the Grandstand. Game as anything. They started battling with the first of the Cardiff mob coming out of the Grange. At first they didn't seem worried about our numbers but then they got legged down Sloper Road as far as the traffic lights, where they regrouped and made another mad stand. For the first time we could see their mob properly in the open road: all the lot from the bus earlier and a few more, a right ragtag and bobtail mob of skins, bikers and all sorts. A chap with a mackintosh and a slashback was up-front adopting a boxing stance. Cardiff didn't hesitate this time and smashed them everywhere. A lot of Millwall got caught by the Ninian Park pub, which was a building site at the time, and Cardiff were whacking with were scaffold clips, timber and anything they could get their hands on. We watched them file back into the station about an hour or so later looking a right sorry bunch. To be honest, Millwall have never brought a full mob to Cardiff. Chelsea were the only ones to give us major problems on our own patch.

In 1976 we played Orient away in the FA Cup third round – and no, we didn't get turned over by Brisbane Road's finest. Let me explain. About 3,000 Cardiff attended that day, many by service train. Again I travelled with IJ and my brother. We got down to Leyton, had our customary pre-match meal of pie and chips and enjoyed a 1-0 Cardiff victory. I've always liked going to Orient. It's one of those places you don't have to look over your shoulder every five minutes.

Back on the Tube after the game everyone was in high spirits as we sped westbound. Who would it be in the next round? Man Utd away? Leeds at home? But as we slowed down coming into Bethnal Green Tube station, things started going badly wrong. The platform was packed tight with the mighty West Ham and they were pissed off because they had just been stuffed 4-0 by Liverpool. The driver had not yet opened the doors. Perhaps he had read the situation and was going to carry on to the next station. We could hear a Cockney voice gleefully screaming, "Cardiff geezers!" With that the doors opened, it seemed in slow motion.

Our carriage must have been less packed than the others as West Ham could lash out with fists and boots with ease. Everybody seemed to have been pushed to either end of the carriage. There was a large space in the middle and West Ham were taking it in terms to stamp on some poor fucker's head. When the Old Bill finally turned up, West Ham just seemed to casually stroll off as if nothing had happened. One thing that has always stuck in my mind about that day was a huge black bloke who was last to leave the train, picking coins out of the pools of blood on the floor. On getting back to Paddington we heard that Cardiff had put up a good fight further down the train but this did not seem to cheer us up after what we had witnessed.

The biggest walkover I've ever seen at Ninian Park came in 1977 with the visit of Everton in a fifth-round FA Cup tie, and a crowd of 34,000. That day the Bob Bank was split down the middle by a very flimsy plastic fence and the Scousers, around 4,000, took up the Canton Stand side. Most of them came on a couple of trains that stopped at the station behind the ground. They didn't seem to have a big mob with them but small groups of a dozen or so. It was around this time that the dressing thing was taking hold in the north west of England and mohair jumpers and straight jeans were very much in evidence amongst the Everton contingent. For Cardiff, it was the trusty donkey jacket and pit boots combination.

During most of the game Cardiff were just walking around the fence and battering Everton senseless. Very few would try to fight back. Those that did seemed to be the beer monster type, not the scallies. Duncan McKenzie's hand-assisted winning goal sparked mayhem. Hundreds of Cardiff started pouring into the Everton section. Many Scousers by now were running down the slope towards the exit gate. From where we were standing we could see that Everton's homebound specials were already in place and seemed to be filling up rather rapidly and it was still only twenty past four. Outside, the police had no real control. By now Cardiff had steamed up onto the platform and were legging Everton across the tracks. A couple got on the train and were terrorising them.

In the late 1990s I was having a drink in the Flying Dutchman in Amsterdam and got talking to a few Everton who had been in Cardiff that day. One claimed it was the worse away game he had ever been to: in his words, "A nightmare from start to finish."

CHAPTER TWO

A Sea of Diamonds and Bright Colours

It was over in a flash.

Forty of them surprised us by jumping off a double-decker bus. We spread into the middle of the road, 15 of us, tops. They bombarded us with missiles in a calculated attack but we stood firm. I was shitting myself but the boys I was with were older and wiser and were relishing the bout.

This lad in a blue Lacoste tee-shirt came bouncing across to lay one on me but I think I surprised him when I stood frozen to the spot and planted a right hook onto his inviting jaw. He went down to his knees. A massive roar went up from the Barry boys, a much-feared contingent of Cardiff City fans, and we ran at this mob in a do-or-die charge. To our great surprise, they legged it everywhere. It didn't make sense. We were outnumbered nearly three to one and some of them were nearly twice the size of me.

By the time the police turned up it was all over and the adrenaline was pumping through my body better than any drug you can imagine. Kevin, one of the Barry boys, came over and congratulated me on my efforts. For a second I thought I was Alan Minter and I grinned like the proverbial Cheshire cat as we walked the half a mile or so to the ground. And that, basically, is a summary of my first active brawl at a football match. It was September 1982, at Walsall; not the most glamorous of locations, admittedly, but I was to find out later on that season that a lot of smaller clubs had decent firms.

I was born in 1965 and was raised in Neath, an industrial town near Swansea. It is a tough place, famous for its ferocious rugby forwards, but there are many genuinely nice people there. Many of them worked in the steelworks at nearby Port Talbot. Football-wise, Neath was split between Cardiff and Swansea fans and the rivalry would occasionally spill over into brawls in the local pubs. There was always a strong faction of about 30 Cardiff from Neath and nearby Glyn-Neath.

City were always a half-decent football team until 1974, when I started watching them. They missed out on promotion to the old First Division in 1971 by a whisker. Then things stared to fall apart. We sold our golden asset, John Toshack, to Liverpool – he later came back to Wales to haunt us at our sworn rivals Swansea – and spiralled to the foot of the Second Division for many years, eventually being relegated to Division Three in May of 1982, a 3-2 home defeat by Luton Town sealing our fate. This was even more heart-breaking due to the fact that Swansea had finished sixth in the top flight.

I had been a football fan from an early age, going to the match with my father. In 1974 I witnessed the first taste of aggro when two waves of blue and white and red and white clashed on the Bob Bank at the now infamous Cardiff City v Manchester United match, then in 1977 when Chelsea and Everton visited Ninian Park, and in 1979 when Stoke City came. I can remember my father telling me to stop watching the violence and concentrate on the football, brainwashing me that those were mindless yobs who had no interest in the game. But by 1981 my father had lost interest and stopped attending, freeing me to go with my mate Gareth and his brother Gus.

At the end of June 1982 the fixtures for the forthcoming season were published and had us travelling to the doldrums of the Football League, places like Wigan, Lincoln, Walsall and Reading. Our first away game was a 4-0 defeat at Leyton

Orient, a typical start for us. It was also on a Tuesday night, so not many of the lads went. Walsall on the following Saturday seemed more appealing.

Cardiff City's crew had started to travel to away games by train by 1982 and Walsall was a nice and easy, relatively short trip. It was a boiling hot morning as 50 boys boarded the train at Neath and Port Talbot, both hotbeds of Cardiff thugs. We were expecting another 100 or so to get on at Cardiff Central but to our surprise around 300 boarded. I felt and looked what I was: a 17-year-old, out of my depth but excited by it all. There were hordes of older, hard-looking bastards who seemed well up for a row. I was impressed. Many of us were wearing the military-style uniform of green flighties (flight jackets) and airwear. We thought we looked the business and were ready for action. The buffet carriage was mobbed with boys drinking themselves into a state as early as 9.30 in the morning. Normal passengers were horrified by the behaviour of some of the Cardiff, chanting and singing their way to the Midlands. Gareth and myself, plus a few of the Neath boys, sat at a table studying the whereabouts of some of the other big firms that day.

Birmingham New Street was, apart from London Euston, probably the most troublesome railway station for football crimes in the country. To our surprise and horror, that day West Brom were playing at home to West Ham United, meaning only one thing: the Inter City Firm (ICF) would be arriving and departing at New Street. If you have been a football lad at any time in your years, you will have bumped into the ICF at least once. These weren't your average lunatics but serious criminals from the notorious East End of London.

As we reached the tunnels of New Street, the whole train went quiet. The beautiful sunshine had been replaced by darkness and every Cardiff fan began to sober up. My heart was racing and my stomach sinking in nervous anticipation. Though we had a major firm on the train that day, the fear of bumping into the ICF started to sink in with the majority of the boys.

When the train eventually stopped, my eyes were fixed to the window, expecting an imminent ambush. Tentatively the doors opened and the barking of police dogs echoed around this dungeon of a place. We proceeded up the escalators, packed like sardines, aware of everything going on around us. There were only five coppers directing us to platform 11. It was around 11.20am and the next train from London was due in at any minute. If they were on it, there would be nothing to stop it going ballistic.

The majority of us that morning were, if we're honest, relieved when an officer informed us that West Ham were already in Smethwick and were planning an ambush on Wolves, who were going to Coventry. So we reached Walsall safely for midday and soaked up the last of that year's glorious summer. Most of the Cardiff boys on the train split up, drinking in the many boozers around the ground with not the slightest fear of any attack from the locals. I got particularly slaughtered on Strongbow, then, with a few others, I had a nose around ten minutes before kick-off. It was then that we fought off the attack from a busload of Walsall described at the start of this chapter.

At the ground we spread the word of our brawl around the away end and were praised endlessly by the Cardiff mob. They were pleasantly surprised to find that Cardiff had a few fighting boys from what was predominantly Swansea City country. The team also performed well and we picked up our first points of the season with a 2-1 victory, with Jeff Hemmerman netting the winner. Our escort back to Walsall station looked impressive, as around 650 Cardiff fans had made the journey up, with over 350 on the train. We looked untouchable as our local train neared New Street again. The inhibitions had disappeared and everyone was well up for a bit of the West Ham if they were about.

I will never forget the next moment as long as I live. As we pulled onto platform 11, I looked to my left and saw a sea of diamonds and bright colours. The platform was chockfull of West Ham; there must have been 700 of them, wearing Pringle jumpers and other sports gear. I was dumbstruck. I had heard all about the most feared firm in the land and was now 50 yards away from them. Our carriage door opened and a huge cry of "Cay-ardiff" echoed around the station. The haunting sound of "I-C-F" bellowed back and a cacophony of words were exchanged. Luckily for us they were well penned in by a wall of police. Some did come through and looked genuinely surprised at the numbers Cardiff had. We were marched across the top of New Street. It was about 5.30pm and the station was packed with Saturday afternoon shoppers. God knows what they made of it all. The police seemed well trained and made little fuss as we were escorted to platform four.

I was a little confused as to why West Ham were dressed up more for the British Open golf tournament or tennis at Wimbledon than in their former hard-looking skinhead image. They had also adopted Spandau Ballet-style wedge haircuts. On the train on the way home I bumped into a couple of the Port Talbot boys and one of them was dressed like the West Ham lot. I asked him what the score was with this new look. He was a fanatical Tottenham fan who travelled with them everywhere, including Europe, and held down a good job with British Steel. He explained that the Cockneys were all starting to dress casually. Many had gone to the 1982 World Cup finals in Spain and robbed the sports shops of their expensive tennis labels such as Ellesse, Fila and Sergio Tacchini. I enquired why some of them looked like golfers and he told me that Pringle jumpers and Farah slacks were in vogue in London especially. From that moment my whole outlook changed. I was already hooked on football violence: now football fashion had a firm grip on me. I'd had an exceptional day out and was hungry for more of the same. Our next away game happened to be Millwall. Say no more.

MILLWALL AT THE Den was and still is a daunting prospect, and the fixture there would be my first visit. I had heard all the grim tales of Cardiff coming unstuck there in the 1970s, so our first meeting for five seasons would be a real test for our firm. The Wall had not had it all their own way. Many reports say they got a rough welcome in the hillsides whenever they travelled to the principality's capital city.

On police advice, the game was to be played on a Sunday afternoon: the thought of hundreds of drunken Taffies besieging South London was not recommended for a Saturday afternoon encounter. In those days the Sunday licensing laws for alcohol were strict, with a 2pm closing time, thus restricting any bouts of drunken trouble. A strong Neath contingent of 16 travelled on the 8am train to meet the supporters' coaches at Ninian Park. There we were hailed by a huge mob of Cardiff's hardcore firm: 400 or so. I boarded coach number eight, which was full of unstable characters who wouldn't have been out of place in *One Flew Over the Cuckoo's Nest.* They were bang up for it. The Barry boys were on our coach and played up all the way to the Elephant and Castle.

When we eventually reached Millwall we were met by a massive police operation. They did not know where Millwall were lying in wait. We got to the coach park and confidently steamrolled off our 17 buses, chanting the latest banter, "Millwall, where are you?" I was a cocksure 17-year-old under the influence of amphetamines and Strongbow, not knowing or caring what Millwall's response would be. Their firm were nicknamed the Bushwhackers, mainly due I believe to the fact that there was a lot of derelict land around the old Den – not dissimilar to *Steptoe and Sons'* back garden – and lots of overgrown weeds and bushes near where our coaches were parked.

A roar of "Millwall" came echoing out of the undergrowth and this 6ft 3in South London docker lunged towards our pack. The shock knocked me for six and within seconds about 40 of South London's worst came wielding metal objects and hurling missiles. Cardiff backed off rapidly at first, leaving a few game lads to take the brunt of their assault. We soon realised that there was only a mob of 40 and Cardiff regrouped and steamed towards these cavemen. I admit that that was the first time my arse fell out of my pants. This was the big time, so we had to show what we were made of. Millwall were the business and stood as about 200 Cardiff ran towards them. A short battle commenced and the Old Bill were soon on our case, letting two police dogs off their leashes.

Inside the Lions' Den the atmosphere became increasingly tense, made worse as Cardiff managed a rare 4-0 away victory. Millwall became agitated as the Bluebirds tore through the heart of their defence. After the match our army of travelling hooligans added to their ire by ridiculing Millwall on either side of the fence.

The Londoners were to have the last laugh. As our coaches headed west after the game, we had just reached the big roundabout by the Elephant and Castle when we were severely ambushed by the Bushwhackers. Only two windows were left on our coach. Obviously this infuriated our mob, who tried to get off the war-torn buses to have a go back. The police lost the plot for a while as 50 Cardiff climbed off their respective transport to pursue the Londoners, who had it on their toes. I could see the point of the ambush but to brick the coaches and then leg it? It seemed pointless. I thought, *surely there must be more of them lying in wait up the old Kings Road?* It was not to be and we were escorted back to South Wales without further trouble but minus our windows. It wasn't a pleasant journey with the raw autumn weather. Still, I was a happy chappie, having witnessed and been actively involved in my first row at the Den. I was also happy to think that I came home to Wales with my newly-donned diamond Pringle jumper intact and my Adidas Forest Hills still sparkling white. My first mission to claim the title of Best Dressed Casual in Wales had come courtesy of my student rail card offer of £10 return from Neath to Paddington a week prior to the Millwall game. After speaking to Parsons and Terry from Port Talbot – two top lads – about quality outlets in London for casual gear, I was prepared for my journey. They told me to target Sharp Sports in Kensington, a haven for tenniswear buyers with such names as Fila, Tacchini, Cerrutti 1881, Ellesse and Adidas Lendl. I splashed out on a sky-blue Tacchini tennis tracksuit, with money that had been given to me as a birthday present to spent on a tacky signet ring or something similar. The tracksuit cost £55, a scandalous price at the time. We were deep in recession under the Margaret Thatcher government, with soaring unemployment, and I was one of the army on the dole. Many Cardiff fans were scraping a living and things would get much worse a few months later when the Miners' Strike began. Like many others, however, I was working three days a week on a fiddle, earning £35 quid to supplement my fortnightly Giro.

My next port of call was Austin Reed on Regent Street, very much an Englishman's country retailers but stocking the best Lacoste around. I purchased a wicked beige V-neck jumper with the very rare white crocodile motif and a black polo neck with a tiny croc emblazoned on the rollneck. I thought I was King Shit leaving the store but was brought down to earth when I was eyeballed across the London street by a Burberry-clad, six-foot coloured gentleman who pursued me as far as Oxford Street, where I managed to leg away through the shopping chaos. He was clearly after my new purchases. London at the time was notorious for young football casuals from other parts of the country being relieved of their new clothes by London firms, mainly Arsenal and West Ham. Thankfully that was the nearest I came to being "taxed" for my naivety. I conquered this threat on subsequent trips by disguising my garments in Top Man or Burton carrier bags and by not wearing any casual gear that would get me sussed. I rounded my shopping trip off that day by purchasing a rare pair of German imported trainers called Adidas Munchen, which to this day remain my favourite trainers.

Those shopping trips of the early '80s were the best because funds were really low and you had to dig out the best to make you look the business. From being behind the times, by the autumn of '82 Cardiff had became one of the best-dressed firms in the country. A lot of Cardiff retailers such as Robert Barker and Austin Reed picked up on the football casual movement and were stocking Lacoste and all the other Italian tennis labels. The city's Austin Reed was later ram-raided and relieved of all its stock on several occasions.

In early October 1982 we had two big home games, Sheffield United and Portsmouth. Both threatened bother on and off the pitch. Our team had struggled early in the season but were now lying in seventh place. We stumbled to a 3-2 home win against new boys Wigan Athletic. At the time they were the only ones to bring any kind of firm to Cardiff that season but unfortunately for the 30 or so Wigan boys who travelled down they found themselves having a good shoeing the length of Tudor Road, mainly instigated by the young Millbank crew from Ely. Hats off to Wigan, they had a go, even though heavily outnumbered.

Sheffield United, by contrast, were disappointing. They came down by coaches and went straight to the ground. Their casual mob was nearly as non-existent as their train mob. At the time most firms were travelling by train due to the great offers British Rail were enticing customers with. Everyone except Swansea City and Sheffield United brought firms on the train. I'm not going to slag the Jacks off for the sake of it but their fighting crew also didn't take full advantage of their

First Division status when Toshack was in charge. Can anyone imagine what the Soul Crew would have been like in their situation? (Incidentally, the nickname Jacks comes from a dog called Jack that was the mascot of a lifeboat crew. It later came to mean a Swansea docker).

Pompey's so-called 6.57 Crew were more tricky and we assembled 200 lads at the Philharmonic pub at 10.30 on the morning of the game. We knew they would bring a firm; in the mid-70s they had been one of the few teams to come on the Grange End, so expectations were high. At 11 o'clock we sent out a few spotters to see if they had arrived. Peter, one of the Ely boys, came running back to the Philly to announce their arrival and we steamed out mob-handed to meet them.

At the corner of Wood Street we were met by at least 400 Pompey, all casually dressed. They saw us at the same time as we saw them and had no hesitation in steaming straight in. We stood firm but more and more of them came flying in and we had to leg back. It was to be one of very few occasions in 20 years that we were legged at home (only Chelsea in '84, Newport County in '87 and Middlesbrough in the '90s ever caused us complete embarrassment at home, and the Newport game was a tie against Merthyr Tydfil at Ninian Park and not a Cardiff game – though that's no disrespect to County's mob that day). One of the top Cardiff lads of all time, Brian Brain, stood on his own and took a hammering. Much to his chagrin, he was also bitten on the arse by a police dog.

A few battles occurred on the way to the ground but it was a token gesture on our part. I still rate Pompey's firm that day to be the most complete mob I've seen at Ninian Park in the 27 years (and counting) that I've been going. That season the 6.57 Crew even tried taking Millwall's infamous seating section, an effort unheard of before. Some years later they had the cheek to walk around Stamford Bridge when Chelsea were at home and Portsmouth were at neighbouring Charlton Athletic, another task deemed impossible at the time. Pompey didn't give a fuck. We all felt totally shamed after the Pompey game. It brought us back down to earth with a bump. Anyone who brings a firm to Cardiff earns a little respect and would normally bear the brunt at the return fixture. Later on that season the proof was to be in the pudding.

CHAPTER THREE

Pass the Dutchie

THE CASUAL SCENE was now sweeping the terraces and every team was developing its own gang of "dressers" – easily identifiable to their rivals but completely inconspicuous to the police, who had not cottoned on to this smart, no-scarves, no-colours look. It was, in many ways, the boom time of soccer hooliganism in Britain. The old mass warfare was being replaced by a new cult of violence: more organised and streamlined.

The season was in full swing and we had even drawn Arsenal in the League Cup, which promised a financial boost for the club as well as a good night out in North London for us. Arsenal were one of the best-dressed firms in the country so we expected a good fashion show to keep us entertained while our team were doubtless getting a thrashing on the Highbury pitch. It was to be the first of three away games in a week and I had to dig hard into my savings to get to all three. Gareth and myself were never ones for going with the official supporters' coaches, but if I was to do the three I had to budget wisely, so Arsenal away would have to be shared with the anoraks.

We got to Highbury to be met by one of West Ham's ICF firm, Taff. He came originally from North Cornelly, in Mid-Glamorgan, and followed Cardiff in the 1970s but was also a West Ham fan. Eventually he left South Wales to seek his fortune in London. There he worked his way up through the

ranks of West Ham's notorious soccer firm to achieve near-
legendary status. He boasted to us that night that he had been
caught up in major scuffles with Arsenal the Saturday previous.
Arsenal v West Ham has always had a bad history of violence
attached to it and Taff, knowing him, would have been right
in the thick of it.

He came to the match with us and the Gooners spotted
him straight away as we entered the Clock End. He became
the subject of a lot of abuse. We were in the middle of the
Clock End with Arsenal on either side of us. Only about 700
Cardiff fans had made the journey due to the league fixtures
taking priority, and of those only about 100 were lads. Most
of the Cardiff unfortunately looked ridiculous due to their
lack of dress sense. Arsenal, of course, were well turned out,
mostly in Burberry and Fila BJ, and it was the first time I
spotted Aquascutum at a match.

There was no real bad feeling at the ground, with many of
their faces opting to find out what had happened at the
Pompey game a week earlier and advising us on some more
quality clothes outlets in the capital. On the pitch we fared
pretty well too, losing only to a late Paul Davies goal, and
afterwards we were escorted to our coaches without any
bother. We heard later on that Taff had been caught by a few
Gunners and given a slap. He always lived by the sword and
this would tragically be his undoing a few years later, when he
apparently "jumped" off a bridge onto a Tube train. Various
stories circulated that just before his death he had fallen out
with some of his West Ham friends over money collected to
pay for their trip to the 1990 World Cup in Italy, but to my
knowledge nothing was ever proven. I had total respect for
him because he always looked out for us and will be
remembered fondly by the majority of my mates.

On the following Saturday, we made the short trip to
Oxford United, being picked up in a Transit van by the
Llanelli Crew. Llanelli is a little pocket town near to Swansea

and a hotbed for Swansea fans, but a firm of 20-odd Cardiff lunatics come from there too. John, a six-foot, ginger-haired monster, has always been there or thereabouts when it has gone off and was the driver that day. We opened the back doors at Neath station and three of his contingent literally fell from the van in a drunken stupor. It was going to be one of those days. We eventually got to Oxford five hours later (it's normally a two-hour journey), being treated on the way to some fine Welsh singing of Musical Youth's "Pass the Dutchie" and the Fat Larry's Band classic "Zoom" which was blaring out of the radio. The average age in the van was about 30, so I felt very young indeed but was treated well by the older boys, who related tales of their Cardiff exploits.

Outside the ground at Oxford we bumped into 40 of their firm waiting on a roundabout. We piled out of the van and ran towards them. They were gone straight away. Reckoning that was the pitiful opposition for the day, we made for a pub and went on the piss. We were disappointed, having heard Oxford had had a big off with Pompey two weeks earlier.

The away end at the Manor Ground was a shitty little open terrace and it seemed about 2,500 Cardiff were packed in, even though legally it held only 2,000. It was chaos. A Hillsborough disaster could have easily resulted. It pissed down all day and just before the game kicked off there was an almighty roar from the Oxford end and a big fight occurred. A handful of Cardiff had gone on their end and were causing mayhem, fronted by Frankie, probably Cardiff's most documented lad of all time. They came back to our end to a hero's welcome, Frankie minus a shoe. He was one of the first football hooligans at Cardiff, famed for such episodes as a huge fight at Paddington Station against Millwall in 1971 when he led a gang clad in *Clockwork Orange* attire, and the occasion he and just one mate attacked a pub of 50 Leeds fans. He even gave magazine and newspaper interviews:

> I go to a match for one reason only: the aggro. It's an
> obsession. I can't give it up. I get so much pleasure
> when I'm having aggro that I nearly wet my pants ... I
> go all over the country looking for it ... Every night
> during the week we go round looking for trouble. Before
> a match we go round looking respectable; then if we see
> someone who looks like the enemy we ask him the time.
> If he answers in a 'foreign' accent, we do him over, and
> if he's got money on him we'll roll him as well.

By the time of the Oxford game he was into his forties but he
still graces the terraces at Ninian Park for big occasions even
now.

We drew the game 2-2 thanks to a last-minute free-kick but
the result didn't stop several hundred Cardiff smashing their
way through side streets of high-quality motors. I condemn
that kind of behaviour and always have. Cardiff (or a few
dickheads who think they're lads) have had a reputation for
this kind of destructive stupidity, similar to the Leeds United
demolition mob that was rampant at the time (Bradford away
in 1985 springs to mind). It is one thing getting tooled up
with weapons for a major row with another firm – though
some mobs baulk at that – but to scare women, children and
normal fans the way they did is a waste of time. A lot of the
main lads will agree. A few bizzies also got wasted that day for
throwing their weight about but that's just the way it goes.

We visited loads of smaller grounds that season, taking
large away mobs by train. They might not seem major scalps
but, in my book, to sustain a reputation you have to go to
these places as well as the Chelseas, Portsmouths and Millwalls.
Bournemouth was the next adventure and was a good laugh.
My friend Stuart and I decided to make a weekend of it and
left early on Thursday morning with an eight-pack of cider.
We fell off the train in Bournemouth and checked into a B
and B not far from the ground. Not surprisingly we were the

first Cardiff to arrive. We sampled a load of the local ale on Thursday night and continued drinking our way through Friday. Like me, Stuart was a big fan of The Specials, and Bournemouth in the early '80s surprisingly proved to be a Mecca of rude boy and Mod memorabilia, so he was over the moon. There were a lot of Scousers working down there in the bars and restaurants and we were made to feel very welcome. By the Friday evening there must have been about 150 of Cardiff's firm on the south coast with another 300 or so travelling on Saturday morning with intentions of staying down on the Saturday night.

Tempers frayed on the Friday night with a lot of the local bouncers mobbing up for a row after refusing entry to many drinking holes. One Cardiff fan was seriously injured by a bouncer, which sparked a major kick-off outside his club that saw several doormen being battered by our ever-increasing firm. On the Saturday morning we had 4-500 lads roaming the streets of Bournemouth without any opposition. Many made their way along the two-mile walk to the ground. An internal row had broken out between a faction of the Port Talbot crew and the Barry boys, resulting in an arranged meet to settle the feud. This was born out of an argument on the train coming down on Friday night and was not uncommon among Cardiff fans, though on this occasion it fizzled out. Because of the pull from such a widespread area of South and West Wales, loads of little firms merge to form an alliance for City, and from time to time internal rows occur between these groups. Unfortunately I once got caught up in a dispute with one of the Port Talbot lot, resulting in a bitter love-hate rivalry for a couple of months. Nowadays our firm seems to act more in unison.

Bournemouth didn't bring any joy on the fight front, so after the game Cardiff went on their predictable rampage through the streets of Boscombe. There were running battles with the police and a few of the local constabulary were hurt.

Leeds United were to repeat this act in 1990, much to the
attention of the national media. In the early '80s it was also
very much the trend to make a few sheckles for one's self by
smash and grab raids on retail outlets. The Scousers were
infamous for their jewellery raids in Europe, and Man United
for their designer clothes heists. So Cardiff, bored of no local
opposition, took it upon themselves to follow suit. Only the
appeal of relieving the proprietor of a sex shop in Bournemouth of his marital aids was more rewarding than a couple
of grams of gold from a jeweller's. I rolled around in laughter
as I witnessed an impressive collection of dildos, love eggs
and top-notch literature being stolen from the shop. The one
that really drew my attention was the life-sized blow-up doll,
happily named Saucy Susan, being held aloft amongst the
cheery Taffies, reminiscent of Bobby Moore's famous picture
parading the World Cup trophy in 1966. The journey home
was a good laugh with plenty of smutty mags doing the
rounds. Steve Scouser, a 20-stone giant from Caerphilly,
surprised no-one by taking home the majority of the Danish
imports; he had a habit of bringing back hardcore porn from
Europe whilst on his trips with Liverpool.

After the hectic week of travelling the country, Cardiff
were treated to a return League Cup tie with Arsenal at
Ninian. This proved to be a lively evening off the pitch.
Predictably Arsenal won the tie 3-1 but the North London
Norty Forty who had made the journey by train were in for a
nasty shock. Before the game, Arsenal had managed to get
themselves an escort and sat the game out in A Block of the
Grandstand. This was becoming increasingly popular amongst
London firms, shunning the terraces for a more comfortable
way of watching the game: sitting down seemed more
appealing than freezing your bollocks off on a windy open
terrace. They were very chirpy and full of themselves and it
was all their main faces making the noise: the likes of Denton,
Miller and Ali Jobe, kindly picked out for us by our Tottenham

contingent, who'd had many battles with them at North London derbies. At the time many of the Cardiff firm watched other clubs around the country and Tottenham had a following from South Wales that included the likes of Mikey, Jacko and Terry, all big fishes at White Hart Lane.

Cardiff's mob decided to leave early. Obviously no major upset was going to happen here and they rested in the Tudor Arms near the railway station, one of Cardiff's main pubs at the time. Within 200 yards of the main station, it was a prime spot for picking off rival fans, as many away supporters who braved the journey to Cardiff had to pass this dump of a pub.

Arsenal walked back to the station. Unbeknown to them and the ten or so bizzies who escorted them, we lay in wait. About 150 Cardiff were in the pub and as the escort came past we steamed across the road. I got put on my backside by some Cockney but despite a bloodied nose I swiftly got back into them. Cardiff were awesome, slapping Arsenal everywhere. I recall Ali from Arsenal holding their firm together but getting nicked. I later met him in my clubbing years when he ran the door for the Flying Records nights at the Soho Theatre Club in London. A very nice chap. I have the utmost respect for him and other footy lads of this nature, totally committed to the row but a true gentleman in conversation. Ali Jobe was shocked that I remembered the battle and told me he received a £100 fine for his efforts. That seems a joke by today's standards. It's quite sad to see the football hooligan seen as little better than a rapist or a paedophile. Agreed, the dickheads who injure or harm innocent bystanders deserve their just rewards but a few boys having fisticuffs are no more villains than a load of sweaty rugby boys slugging it out on the pitch. While I'm on my soapbox, every year in Cardiff we play host to several big rugby occasions and the behaviour of the rugby fans is on a par with anything that football fans get up to but is ignored and even laughed at by the authorities and the local constabulary. We see it, and some of the things they get away with you wouldn't believe.

We were not favoured too highly in North London, by Arsenal anyway, after that. It came to light a few weeks later that some Cardiff lads in the first leg at Highbury had bumped into a dozen or so Gunners on the border of a council estate in Finsbury Park, resulting in several Arsenal being striped (slashed) and the theft of their swanky Tacchini Dallas and Fila Borg tracksuit tops. As well as that, a fine selection of P-funk and Philly 12-inch singles were requisitioned, a few of which came my way and were included in my DJ sets later on. A few years later, when Cardiff were travelling up North, a few unfortunate City lads bumped into Mr Denton and Co., on their way to an Arsenal fixture at Stoke. The heavily outnumbered Cardiff firm were relieved of all their bespoke garments. I don't suppose they have forgiven us for beating them at Wembley in 1927 either, thus becoming the only team to take the FA Cup out of England!

CHAPTER FOUR

The New Street Horrors

AFTER SEVERAL TRIPS to London and Manchester, I was a head-to-toe, fully-fledged football casual. It became an obsession. Funds were still tight, so to enable us to buy new we had to sell or swap the old garments, common practice amongst the casuals. I was starting to favour the northern dress sense of semi-flared jeans, German imported Adidas trainers – preferably Trimm Trabb or Munchen – and jeans, and the tracksuit was replaced by suede jackets or Harris tweed. These were good times and our firm was rated one of the best in the country, especially for the numbers we took away by train.

One cold and miserable November Saturday I got myself out of bed at the unearthly hour of 5am to board the first train to Cardiff from Neath. I should have been used to the early starts due to the fact that I now worked for peanuts for the General Post Office but it still needed several cups of piss-poor British Rail coffee to wake me up. I thought I looked the dog's in my new C&A hooded suede coat. Don't laugh: C&A was the Mecca between 1982 and 1984 for suede garments favoured mostly by the Scousers and Mancs. At Cardiff station I was pleasantly surprised to find about 350 Soul Crew waiting for the train for our trip to Lincoln, which would take us via the deadly Birmingham New Street station.

Despite all the rumours over the years, the name Soul Crew was adopted by Nicky P, an ex-Spurs and Cardiff lad

who came up with the moniker in recognition of many Cardiff
fans' love of soul music, with bands at the time like Central
Line, D-Train, Shalamar, Shakatak, Parliament and George
Clinton. Don't quote me, but I think a fringe mob of
Tottenham adopted the name "Soul Firm" in the late '70s,
but Cardiff were the original and only Soul Crew. Anyway,
the name stuck and is still widely used today. I was still very
much a junior as older mobs from Llanrumney (a massive
council estate), Ely and a large contingent of the young, up-
and-coming Docks crew boarded the train. Considering the
tortuous journey ahead – we had to change three times to
finally reach Lincoln – this was a good turnout.

On the train we scanned the newspapers for a look at who
was travelling where. Much to our liking, we saw that
Birmingham City were going to Derby County and we were
due to bump into the Zulus on New Street. Cardiff had a
reputation of being big drinkers and most of our mob was
already pissed by the time we got to Gloucester station. The
unruly behaviour of our firm forced the British Rail buffet
staff to close early. Despite this, in those days you were rarely
greeted by British Transport Police and little attention was
brought upon us, thus not stifling the plans we were hatching
for Birmingham.

Eventually we arrived at New Street – Battleground Central
– and got off with little fuss. We were surprised to find that
there were no bluenoses hanging about. Then we realised that
we had to go to Derby to change to our final destination at
Lincoln. Slightly bewildered at the absence of Brummies, we
boarded our train, but just as it was about to pull off, a mass
of Tacchini and Pringle-clad young Zulus appeared and got
on. There were about 150 of them and they had obviously
delayed their arrival until the last minute. Why? I suspect they
had got wind that we were coming through, had not noticed
most of our mob congregated down at the bottom end of the
vast platform and had just seen the few in full view of the

escalators. Birmingham must have seen these 30 or so Welshmen and then braved it thinking that was our mob in total. Much to their shock we outnumbered them nearly three to one. Even more surprisingly, nothing happened on the train, not even a cross word. Some chatted and even played cards together. What was going on?

We got to Derby station and for a moment went our separate ways. Birmingham climbed the stairwell and we moved along the platform awaiting the arrival of the Lincoln train. All of a sudden I heard a roar and Birmingham came flying down the adjacent staircase, punching anyone in sight. We backed off at first, surprised at their action but soon realised what was going down. We regrouped, proceeded towards the sly Brummies and steamed them off the platform. A few disgruntled Zulus sought refuge by running across the railway tracks.

Although we heavily outnumbered them, this was to be a defining moment in the history of the Soul Crew. The news spread like wildfire across the country, much to the ridicule of the Zulus. We had to bear in mind these were the days before the very violent Caribbean contingent had begun to grace the St Andrews terraces, but when a club in the First Division playing 50 miles up the road was routed by a club from the depths of the League playing 300 miles away, it spoke volumes for us.

The fun wasn't over. We arrived at Lincoln not long before the kick-off so there wasn't time to have a beer. The Old Bill presence had swelled dramatically due to the attention we had brought upon ourselves at Derby station. Lincoln also had a welcome committee for us, having heard of our reputation, and were doing their best to infiltrate our sizeable escort. We were cock-a-hoop and deemed ourselves invincible for our efforts earlier on in the day.

About 50 of us became very cheeky and decided to go into their seats in the main stand. Nicky P was rounding everyone up for a pitch invasion at the end of the game. We had some good lads in the seats that day; many of them followed other clubs at the time in the First Division like Spurs, Villa, West Ham and Liverpool, but when Cardiff were playing a fixture away from home they more often than not went to these unconquered territories. The big thing at the time was to do the 92 league grounds and many South Wales pro-Cardiff lads who followed other clubs managed this remarkable achievement. One lad, James, did all 92 in two seasons.

The final whistle went and the mob in the seats ran onto the unguarded pitch. We headed straight to the Lincoln end, taunting them to join us on the pitch. They needed no invitation. The whole end seemed to make a beeline to our 50 overconfident Soul Crew. Much to our dismay a mob of around 400 surrounded us and surged in, punching and kicking anything in their way. This was not supposed to happen after our achievements on Derby station and, boy, did it bring us down to earth. We took a savage beating.

I ended up scrapping with a Lincoln fan who punched me clean on the jaw. The next thing I can remember is being brought round in the Lincoln City dugout. How ironic football hooliganism is: one minute you're Mike Tyson, the next you're Mickey Mouse. In fairness, Cardiff lads on the terraces were fighting with stewards and police to come to our rescue. I came away badly bruised but proud I had stood firm with the older boys, and was highly praised on our seven-hour journey home to South Wales. Nicky and a few of the others cut a few Lincoln up before he had his new Armani top torn off his back.

After that I never took any away fixture for granted. I realised that our reputation was growing and we would be met at all levels with a firm wanting to match ours. The only place I took things out of context was at Swansea in 1984 but that's another story. Next up was the FA Cup. We had been relegated the previous season to the old Division Three so this meant us playing from the first round with all the non-league clubs. The first round of the FA Cup to me was one of the highlights of the hooligan calendar, alongside the third round and the first and last games of the season. It pitted the local village side against the league big boys, with memories of Hereford's Ronnie Radford 30-yard screamer against Newcastle and Dicky Guy's superb penalty save for then non-league Wimbledon against the mighty Peter Lorimer of Leeds United. The draw was made and we were to make the short trip to Wokingham, a small town on the outskirts of Reading. In my mind this was a potential upset. We weren't taking the off-field activities for granted either. We knew that, with Wokingham being so close to Reading, there was a probability that either Chelsea or West Ham would turn up. Reading was a nursery for big London clubs and especially the aforementioned.

Gareth decided to hitchhike to Wokingham because funds were tight. I had been put off hitchhiking after a shocking experience two years earlier, when Gareth and I had decided to try the impossible feat of getting to Grimsby. I'd been advised by Gareth that we would have no problem because he had achieved it the season before and came home on the supporters' club coach free of charge, thus only spending a tenner on the whole trip, but unfortunately I must have been a bad omen because we only managed to reach Bridgend before we gave up. I opted for the train to Wokingham with Guss, Pickle and Gorey.

We caught up with Gareth outside the tin-shack ground just before kick-off, having opted to have a few beers in Reading. He informed us that a few City boys had been slapped by local skinheads thought to have been Chelsea and that their mob was in a boozer just up by the ground. *En route* to the ground we bumped into a few more Cardiff and told them what had happened, so we went to have a look for this mob. As we reached their pub, a few of them were drinking

outside and realised what was happening. They withdrew to
the pub to get the rest, then came out mob-handed throwing
glasses and barstools. We backed off a few yards and had a
stand-off in the middle of the road. Punches were exchanged
until the police rounded us up and took us to the ground. A
few of the boys from Barry got nicked and were later made to
pay hefty fines.

Ten minutes from the end of the game we were looking
certain to go out of the Cup after Wokingham had taken a
shock lead. The only segregation was a flimsy fence and the
Chelsea mob, 40-strong, were adjacent to us. If we were going
out, the only thing to do was to try to get the game abandoned
by invading the pitch. So without further ado we climbed the
perimeter fences onto the mud bath of a field. It looked very
impressive as we steamed towards Chelsea's horrified faces.
In fairness they were up for it and a battle occurred on the
pitch. We were eventually herded back onto the terrace,
having succeeded in holding up the game for about 20 minutes,
but our attempts to get it abandoned failed.

Dillwyn, a character from Llantwit-Major who could write
a book on his own about his antics at matches, managed to
stay on the pitch and proceeded towards the bemused referee
and linesman, who were waiting safely in the centre circle for
the trouble to die down. He managed to confiscate the match
ball from the officials and tried doing a spot of keepy-up, to
the pleasure of our cheering mob. The police eventually
rugby tackled him, to the laughter and applause of the home
supporters. Picture the scene: a 6ft 4in, ginger-headed,
bespectacled lunatic covered from head to toe in mud.
Eventually the game resumed and the "time out" for the
players seemed to favour the Cardiff team as they scrambled
a last-minute equaliser from David Tong. We won the replay
comfortably but were knocked out in the next round by non-
league Weymouth after surrendering a two-goal lead. No
pitch invasion that time though.

Much to the annoyance of the Thames Valley Police, we were back in Berkshire later that month for a league meeting with Reading. This night fixture appealed to a lot of our firm because it was a relatively short 75-minute train journey. To my amazement we had about 450 lads on the train alone and shocked the locals with our behaviour on route to Elm Park. Reading's ground has one of the longest walks from the railway station and Cardiff besieged and ransacked many local corner shops and off licences on the way. Inside the ground, 30 lads got onto Reading's end and it went off for ages, two minutes at least, with Melvin from Barry getting a bit of a rough deal for his efforts.

By Christmas of 1982 we were sitting pretty at the top of Division Three. On Boxing Day we beat local rivals Newport County 3-2. At the time, Newport put up very little opposition, rowing-wise at least, and after a lively battle at Home Park, Plymouth, on New Year's Day, resulting in 30 Cardiff arrests, 1983 looked good to be an eventful year on and off the pitch.

CHAPTER FIVE

The Big One

WITH FA CUP third-round day no longer of interest after our humiliation against Weymouth, we had to concentrate on promotion. This wasn't a bad thing; after all, we could now fulfil our home league fixture against Millwall. On the morning of the game we left Neath with a full squad of 25 lads. You could always gauge a big game from the numbers that would go from Neath. It had snowed the previous night and the ground was rather frosty. As we arrived early at Cardiff Central we heard rumours that the game might be postponed. Some of the lads went straight to the Great Western Hotel, a pub used by most of our mob mainly due to its location about 100 yards from the train station. I made a beeline for the January sales and picked up a rather natty cashmere jumper from Howells that knocked me back £40.

After my shopping expo I returned to the Great Western to find a pub full of unstable gentlemen from both the Rhondda and Rumney Valleys. Terry from Port Talbot clocked an old (to us) bloke in the corner drinking on his own, sporting a Dye cap and reading *The Sun*. To any onlooker he just seemed a normal early-doors pisshead scouring the paper for some winners at that day's race meetings. The guy was in his forties and Terry informed us that he was a spotter from Millwall. I greeted this with great amusement and said, 'There's no way he's a football lad.' Later that day I was to eat a great slice of humble pie, as it turned out he was there to suss out our numbers for the arriving Millwall firm.

That day I witnessed the best mob of Cardiff I had seen in ten years I had been watching the City. We had at least 6-700 lads waiting in the Great Western and the Albert. Throughout my story I do not exaggerate numbers; there is no point in bullshitting you. I admit when we got done and swear these numbers are a true.

Andy from Penarth broke the news that the game had been postponed due to the weather. We were devastated. In the back of my mind I think the police had seen the size of our firm and advised Cardiff City Football Club to call the game off to save them a big job. Ironically it was the only game to be called off throughout the fixture list that day.

Were Millwall going to still turn up unaware of the circumstances? Parsons came up with a top idea of gate-crashing the Newport County-Everton cup tie at Somerton Park. It seemed such a shame to waste this mob on an all-day bender around Cardiff so we recruited about 200 or so for the short journey to Newport. In the meantime about 60 Millwall had turned up at Cardiff Central surrounded by a heavy police presence. A few of us liased with the Cockneys to get it sorted in Newport. The Old Bill were not clued up to our plans and while they tried to protect Millwall from our pack, we slipped through the net and headed for Gwent.

Simon, one of our lads who later had a big influence at Ninian Park, managed to chat with a couple of Midlands-based Millwall who had arrived earlier that morning. He informed us that they were up for joining up with Cardiff to have a go at the Scousers when we got to Newport. We put the idea to the rest of the lads but it was swiftly rejected, as we had a mob more than capable of doing Everton on our own. Everton were still haunted by the 1977 hiding dished out to them at Ninian Park.

We arrived at Newport and stalked the streets looking for

both County and Everton. A few Scousers passed in a Transit and assumed we were Newport. Much to their dismay, a roar of "Cardiff!" echoed around the Newport side street. They retreated to their van and a Sweeney-style getaway occurred as we chased it up the street. The traffic lights turned to red and we caught the van only for it to speed through the red light, nearly crashing into an oncoming vehicle.

In the meantime, Millwall had twigged that we had gone to Newport and followed us there. We arrived at the ground and went straight for the Everton end. Confusion reigned as police tried segregating us from the Scousers. I expected a big firm of Everton but was surprised to find only 500 travelling fans and just a handful of good lads. They were equally shocked at what was happening and many of them bottled it and hid from us behind a cordon of police.

At about 3.30pm a mob of Millwall arrived at the ground, lead by a six-foot black geezer. The potential for an almighty row was brewing. Because we had knocked back Millwall's request to join up they were champing at the bit and decided to have a go at us. One small away terrace had Millwall, Everton and Cardiff – with flimsy segregation between the three – all waiting to go off. Fisticuffs started flying between Millwall and Cardiff. By now Everton wanted to join up with the Cockneys to do us. We were backed off into a corner but battled our way back to the middle of the end. We did well that day with the 40 lads who had made it into the ground against over 120 Cockneys and Scousers who saw fit to join in.

We left at half-time and, much to our surprise, were not given an escort back to Newport station, so we decided to stop in town for a drink. After the game Everton's escort came back to the station. We got wind that they were on platform three and had another go at them. The police were now on top but couldn't stop us as Everton backed off and retreated to their waiting train. All in all, a good result for Cardiff.

By March 1983, City were in a promotion place. Our nearest rivals battling for the top three places were Huddersfield Town, Pompey and Newport County. We had to play all three within two weeks. Huddersfield were first at Ninian Park, with both teams sharing the spoils in a 1-1 draw. They brought a coach full of boys, headed by Clarence, a six-foot beret-wearing coloured lad who was one of the gamest I have ever come across. They saw fit to try to take the Ninian Park pub and did pretty well for a while, only to be heavily outnumbered by our mob. One Cardiff fan was stabbed that night but due to sheer numbers we eventually legged Huddersfield down Wellington Street.

Next up was the Big One: Portsmouth away, the only fixture that rivalled Millwall for the newly-named Soul Crew. The night before the game, I celebrated my eighteenth birthday in a wine bar in Neath along with all the local boys. Some of the Cardiff lads made the journey down West to get me bladdered and I was in such a stupor that I nearly missed the big day.

Thirty-five lads from Neath and Glyn-Neath were at Neath station on Saturday morning, our biggest turnout to date. This was an unthinkable amount of support, especially so near to Jackland. By the time the train reached Cardiff, there were at least 200 boys already on it, with 60 or 70 from Bridgend and over 100 from the Pure Violence Mob (PVM) from Port Talbot, headed by Terry and "Tom Jones" (not the singer). Tom achieved legendary status at Ninian Park. He was a small half-caste lad from Grimsby who had moved to Port Talbot and was to be Public Enemy Number One in Swansea for much of the late '80s and early '90s, mainly because he had beaten up many of their firm one-to-one, which annoyed the Gypos (a name given to Swansea by us due to the lack of dress sense and because of a film based in the Swansea area called *Twin Town*). Llanelli also had a big contingent on the train that day, headed by Mr English. This mob alone would have gone through most firms, even before we were met by another 500 waiting at Cardiff Central. The casual movement was at its peak and had taken hold of the Soul Crew, with all but a few of the travelling mob dressed to the nines. We looked like an army waiting for battle.

The Portsmouth Harbour train left platform one at 9am. Thirteen carriages were packed with fighters. Pompey would not know what had hit them. They'd had a result in Cardiff earlier in the season so we were well up for revenge and confident of getting it. All the old faces were out and for the first time in my years I could have even seen us doing the business at Chelsea or West Ham with the numbers we had. Sadly it was a dry train with no buffet car serving alcohol. At Newport station another 100 lads got on and by the time we got to Bristol Temple Meads they had to put another three carriages on due to the swelling numbers of Soul Crew. One of the bizzies on the train told us that police in Cardiff station radioed through to him that another 600 lads were behind us, coming on the next train, which was leaving Cardiff at 10am. Now this was ridiculous. We had managed to muster every lad who had ever watched Cardiff and had over 1,000 on our way to the South Coast. Ask any Pompey lad who was there on that warm March afternoon and he won't dispute it.

We arrived at midday. I was feeling nauseous from the previous evening's alcoholic binge but nothing was going to stop me with the adrenaline pumping through my veins. This was the pinnacle of what I wanted to achieve, they very thing I looked forward to the most. It might seem incomprehensible to non-hooligans, but this was what we lived for.

The Old Bill (OB) presence was immense and we were escorted through the back streets to the ground. Steve Scouser summed up the events in a nutshell. "We've got to many here to do anything," he yelled. He was right. We needed too get a splinter group of 100 or so to break the escort and search for Pompey's mob. This has been the Soul Crew's undoing many times over the years: they have so many different mobs that it is very difficult to organise. People who have tried to "steer the ship" have been muscled out for wanting to be top dog, but with the amount of boys to handle we needed guidance. The confusion has, however, had the advantage of making it difficult for the Old Bill to pinpoint or dawn-raid the Soul Crew because of the sheer numbers; even the "normals" who don Cardiff City shirts are up for the ruck.

Pompey proved at least before the game to be a giant fuck-up. The police sussed what was happening and took us straight to the ground. By 12.30 we were outside the turnstiles at Fratton Park. At that moment, I wished I had stayed in bed nursing my hangover. Yuan and myself decided to watch the match from the seats, enjoying the sight of our impressive away contingent. But as the ground filled up, we were surrounded by some of the 6.57 Crew. Instead of giving us a hiding, they decided to have a chat with us to see what was going to happen after the game. Strange as it may seem to the uninitiated, there seems to be an unwritten rule at football these days about etiquette and respect for other mobs. Pompey certainly fall into this bracket. It would have been easy for them to fill us in and gain no brownie points but to their credit they tried getting it organised *en masse*. They were also very interested in talking about clothes and told us that they were adopting the smarter Armani knitwear for the next summer. They were impressed by our numbers and were surprised we hadn't put more of a fight up at Ninian Park. We informed them that we were disgraced by that day and were here to make amends.

At the final whistle we were relieved to get away with a priceless point after a drab goalless draw; if Bob Hatton had grabbed the goal he should have scored at the end, we could have been in pole position for promotion. Yuan and I then witnessed the inevitable riot. We had 3,000 fans in the ground with an estimated 1,200 lads. Pompey's firm, mostly congregated on the open terrace opposite us, had to leave the ground via a back alley behind the away end (much like the set-up at Ninian Park with the Bob Bank and Grange End). Stones were thrown from neighbouring gardens into the away end and City fans retaliated by hurling them back, resulting in one of our mates from Swansea, John, a City diehard, getting kayoed. Incensed City fans then started ripping off the hands of the famous Portsmouth clock, a relic that had been at Fratton Park since their heyday in the 1930s. Police tried containing the raging City and a massive row with the OB started. Chunks of the crumbling terracing were hurled back at Pompey, and Neath legend Brian Brain even managed to find a plank of timber and launched it into a pack of 6.57. Eventually the Old Bill got us out of the ground and escorted us to Fratton station, a safer option than walking us the two miles back to Central station.

We had sought revenge all season for what happened in Cardiff and this was our golden opportunity. The escort back to the train reached 1,500 or so, a mob which looked deadly. Portsmouth tried their best to get at us, steaming down several side streets but we were not budging. Every side street to Fratton station was full of them – they must have had the same numbers as us – and finally we had it with them outside the railway station and backed them off down the road. Their ringleaders were furious with them but this was our finest hour and revenge was sweet. It reached anarchy level and the OB lost it for a while and only regained order by letting the dogs from their leads.

On the train on the way home we laughed with the release of tension and swapped battle stories. Our mood became euphoric with the news that the Jacks had been relegated. If we gained promotion, we would be playing them in the league for the first time in four seasons. It was all a far cry from the previous season, when we were doomed for the drop while the Jacks beat the likes of Man Utd, Liverpool and Leeds and had been serious contenders to win the league.

CHAPTER SIX

The First Picture of Summer

PROMOTION WAS SECURED by an individual strike by Dave Bennett against Leyton Orient in a 2-0 home win. The party began. On the pitch the rewards were sweet. A short stay in Division Three was okay, we had been to the Lincolns, Readings and Leyton Orients, now bring on Leeds, Man City, Pompey (again) and Birmingham. The week before the end of the season, we completed our away fixtures at league new boys Wigan Athletic.

Earlier in the season a few Wigan had had a difficult time in Cardiff. Now it was our turn to go to the rugby league town. About 300 lads made the awkward journey by train. This, apart from the big games, was the best mob of Cardiff I had seen all season. All the main faces were there. We settled down to a few beers in a boozer near the railway station. Steve and Mikey went for a wander and stumbled across a pub called the Bee's Knees, where Wigan had about 150 lads who wanted a row. Gareth and myself went to a chippy and bumped into one of their boys. He turned out to be Russ, one of their best-known figures and also a face at Man U. His jaw was wired from a major fracas at Wembley the week before: he had run into a mob of Scousers and come off considerably worse. We chatted for a while and he advised us that they would meet Cardiff at the top of the high street for a row. This was the first arranged row I had been involved in, bearing in mind there were no mobile phones or Internet arrangements in the early '80s. It was purely trial and error.

Cardiff were confident of overturning these northerners and marched up the street mob-handed. We were surprised at Wigan's casual presence and at how up for it they were, as they stood firm at the top of the hill. A big row took place and after much battling we managed to budge them. Apart from Millwall and Portsmouth, they had proven to be the sternest opposition we had come across all season. Inside the ground, some Cardiff came unstuck in Wigan's end. About 30 or so lads who obviously didn't have any respect for the locals started gobbing off and regrettably paid the price. One Cardiff fan was stretchered away unconscious.

Over the past ten years I have personally formed a lifelong friendship with some Wigan lads. One of them is even godfather to my daughter, Victoria. For a small town, I can't believe how many lads they can pull and a Cardiff-Wigan alliance is very prominent these days. I have also bumped into Russ on many occasions since and chatted about the old days and some of their firm I have the utmost respect for.

We finished the 1982-3 season with a local derby at Bristol Rovers. These were the days when Rovers owned their own ground at Eastville. Cardiff had had many battles with them in the '70s and we weren't expecting anything different on the penultimate day of the season, as the three-mile walk from Bristol Temple Meads station to Eastville has brought a number of memorable rows.

We arrived early enough that Saturday morning to bump into a large mob of Bristol City on their way to Swindon Town. There were 100 waiting for us but our mob of 500 Soul Crew ensured that the Robins had their feathers well and truly clipped. It got so outrageous that we got bored of chasing them along the Avon embankment.

The carnival atmosphere ensured a good day and many City lads had opted for traditional fancy dress. On the pitch we drew 1-1 but unfortunately lost our main striker, Jeff

Hemmerman, just before half-time. A broken leg prematurely ended his career. This was even more frustrating due to the fact we had already been promoted and there was no need to play him. This was a massive blow both for player and team.

Towards the end of the game, someone spotted that the gates to the home supporters' terrace were open. Word got around and five minutes before the final whistle a mob of 70 or so met outside in the car park behind the Cardiff end. At the time it was in vogue to turn up on the home supporters' end with only minutes of the game left and a few of the older heads followed suit. Before we knew it we were amongst the Wurzels and all hell let loose. I was kicked and punched several times and was briefly concussed. We had a toe-to-toe with Rovers for about five minutes and eventually penned them into a corner of their end. A massive surge from the Cardiff end resulted in the perimeter fence being dismantled and a few lads spilled onto the pitch. This was not uncommon at Eastville: Chelsea a few seasons earlier had fought running battles with the local constabulary. This day also witnessed the first police horses at a match in the UK.

The rowing spilled into the car park. In the confusion, Neath Punk dismantled his studded belt and proceeded to whack anyone in his way. Unfortunately he vented his anger on a Sergio Tacchini-clad young man called Lug, a Villa fan from Cardiff. I persuaded them to stop fighting and explained that both parties were Cardiff. From our point of view, the disturbance had finished the season off in style. The news also came through that we were finally going to play the Jacks in a league game next season; their bubble had burst and the Swansea v Cardiff league game was one of many to look forward to.

The long hot summer of 1983 was a gem. The weather was superb, one of the hottest since 1976, and the casual movement was at its peak, with *The Face* magazine carrying the first big article on the new fashion phenomenon written by Kevin

Sampson, who I later met at several gigs when he managed The Farm. His four-page feature was dedicated to the West Ham Under-Fives. There was even a pop band that year (QPR fans) who donned casual gear. I can't for the life of me remember their name but they were absolutely garbage. More shops in South Wales were stocking the casual range. Unfortunately for them, they were being relieved of that stock by high-tech ram-raids by crews from Llanrumney and the Docks. We had got wind that Porthcawl Golf Club had been stripped bare of its Pringle and Burberry range and for the rest of the summer most of Cardiff's West Glamorgan contingent could be seen in Burberry check. I was very much a hat man at the time and was a subject of much ridicule by unstreetwise Neath youngsters for donning my Sherlock Holmes-style deerstalker, much favoured by the Scousers in 1981. Looking back I would probably have laughed myself if I'd have been one of them and seen someone walking down the street with a deerstalker and blue Pringle jumper.

In June 1983, Gareth and myself, bored of hanging around Neath waiting for the next season, darted off to Amsterdam to seek some rare Adidas footwear. We were tight on budget and took advantage of a cheap, chartered coach trip. For a moderate £49 we could get an overnight stay in the sex capital of Europe. We had also heard that the Trimm Trabb and Munchen in a wide selection of colours were waiting to be snapped up. Sixteen hours later we arrived and went on the hunt for the clobber, only to find that Scousers had robbed the place blind the previous week whilst on a pre-season tour of Holland. Instead we both got smashed on the strange local gateaux, had a tour of the red light district and giggled all the way home to Neath, in good spirits but alas with no vintage footwear.

After a few days we got itchy feet again and decided to take advantage of another great offer. Throughout that summer, British Rail were running trips from Port Talbot, Neath and

Swansea to Rosslaire in Southern Ireland for a mere £10
ferry/train journey. This was too good to turn down. For an
extra £5 you could get a train transfer from Rosslaire to
Dublin. We worked out the timetables (we were now experts
at planning our routes in the UK during the football season)
with no high expectations of coming back with bagfuls of
bespoke clothing but thought it would be a good piss-up. We
had a few beers in the Duke of Wellington in Neath before
heading off for the 11.30pm train on a Friday night. The
Duke was a great pub where all the Neath Blues would drink.
It had plenty of top women to chat up and a jukebox that was
second to none. We were big on New Order and Echo and the
Bunnymen at the time. As we left the pub our favourite tune
of that year was bellowing out of the battered old jukebox,
and any time these days I hear the track "The First Picture of
You" by the Lotus Eaters, I smile, because it reminds me of
our trips to Dublin.

Our journey was fuelled with Guinness as we shared the
boat with about 600 Paddies on the way home from holidaying
in the UK. After eight hours sailing we boarded the train to
Dublin, pissed out of our brains, and arrived in Dublin at
11am, giving us seven hours shopping time in the Irish capital.
The temperature soared to 85 degrees plus. We were barely
there ten minutes when we stumbled across a huge department
store. We noticed it had a rack of Chemise Lacoste. The
average price at the time in the UK for a plain, polo-style tee-
shirt was £35-plus. In Dublin they were less that half the
price. Our eyes bulged out of our heads and I soon sobered
up, with pound-note signs running through my head. We
bought virtually all their stock of jackets, tee-shirts and
jumpers, and a large Head bag to bring them all home in.
Because Southern Ireland was not part of the UK it meant
that all quality European labels were at European prices so we
repeated the exercise on several more occasions that summer,
making a handsome "raise" in the process. However, once

again the Scousers had beaten us to all the best trainers in Dublin. We had gathered the fact that there were green Trimm Trabb knocking about and searched every Dublin sports shop but to no success.

At the start of the 1983-84 season Cardiff must have had the largest contingent of Lacoste-clad fans in the league. The pre-season fixtures were issued and a very interesting little game at Llanelli looked appealing to the Neath Crew. Llanelli is only six miles from Swansea and a passionate hatred exists between Neath and Llanelli folk. As we had plenty of spare time in those days, a few of us went on the piss in Swansea on the day of the game. We met up with another 15 or so Cardiff at the ground, giving us a total of 40 lads. The game was simply irrelevant to us as we noticed about 25 or so boys at the other end of the ground who were obviously Jacks being nosey. They started gobbing off and, in fairness, were well up for a row and started mingling in with us. One of their lads was called Foster and I have had several run-ins with him over the years. All was strangely calm for two minutes, then one of their skinheads punched me from behind and all hell broke lose. One of our lads, Nigel, probably the hardest lad I know, smacked one of the skinheads and knocked him out. A wicked off occurred and, as I was punching one of their boys, a skinhead girl attacked me from behind. I turned around and knocked her out, not knowing it was a girl. I felt terrible at the thought of knocking a woman out and tried to help her but when she regained consciousness she was up for fighting again, so I switched my attention to one of their lads.

It took 20 minutes for the violence to calm down and then only because the local constabulary had turned up. At one moment during that row I had been seriously worried because I thought I had killed the girl. The teams were taken off the pitch and the row spilled out onto the streets. The Jacks were still having a go but we were now in fifth gear and eventually whacked them up the road. A considerable write-up in the local paper led to an undercover police operation to try to bring down our firm. That, to this day, was one of the wildest rows I have ever been involved in at a match. All of our 40 or so lads were rowing. Normally you would find about 50% would be fighting in any football row and the other 50% trading insults or taking photographs. It was to be a very eventful season.

CHAPTER SEVEN

The Ultimate Season

I MISSED THE first game of the 1983-84 season at Charlton because of a family wedding. Five hundred City made the trip, with about 200 on the train. A 2-0 defeat didn't give us the start we had hoped for and a few City fans even fought amongst themselves. This spilled over to our first home game against Man City. Things had been brewing between a few of the lads from Grangetown and a main face called Nicky P, who had been trying to muscle in and take over the Soul Crew. The Grangetown took umbrage. Rumour had it that Nicky had extreme right-wing tendencies, which did not go down well with some of the lads, in particular a top boy of Mediterranean extraction known as Bubble. Nicky was also trying to turn the Soul Crew into a "casuals only" firm and to get rid of anyone who didn't wear the gear but we had quite a few respected rowers who did not want to dress that way and that led to further tension.

It came to a head in the Grandstand at the City game. Nicky was blamed for a cock-up at Portsmouth the previous season when he said he knew where their firm were drinking, only to lead the lads onto a dodgy council estate where we were all promptly rounded up by the police. Bubble had the last say on the matter and after the City game we would never see Nicky again. He was a very controversial character but I thought he was okay. He had good organisational skills and with a mob our size we needed a front man, but he didn't do himself any favours with his political views. In fact any person who has tried to organise Cardiff's disparate firms has always been knocked off his perch.

Man City was potentially one of the biggest games that year but they failed to impress by only bringing 30 lads on the train. The Ely mob, fronted by Peter M, swiftly chased City back onto the platform they had just come off. That was the only entertainment that day, off the pitch anyway, but we managed a good 2-1 win, with my old school colleague Paul "Sharky" Bodin netting both goals. Paul managed to sort me out some freebies that season, which were very welcome.

Our first major venture away was Leeds. They had been relegated from the top flight the season before and were one of the best mobs in the country, with a massive away following. They were known as the Service Crew because they preferred to travel on ordinary "service" trains rather than the heavily-police "football specials." We took a cracking mob of 350-plus to Yorkshire by train that September afternoon. Another 200 or so lads went by private coaches and another 100 or so in cars, totalling more than 600 who were up for it. As we arrived at Leeds the home lads were spotting us from their boozer, the Prince of Wales, and seemed shocked to see how many lads we had on the service train. They made a feeble attempt to break the Old Bill escort as we were walked the one and a half miles to Elland Road.

The only incident that day came when Bubble's coachload got onto the Leeds end but they were sussed by the police as they entered the ground. They had been drinking in the Peacock across the road from the home end and said Leeds made no attempt to budge them from their boozer. Mind you, this was 50 of our top firm. After the game the police put us on four double-decker buses back to the station. Leeds made an attempt to ambush us *en route* by launching bricks from a hillside opposite the ground, smashing several windows on the buses. They were also waiting in the buffet area of the railway station and a skirmish broke out between 20 or so of their Wakefield Crew and a few of us. I was lucky not to get nicked as the Old Bill grabbed a Leeds fan instead of me in a case of mistaken identity. Leeds were all wearing flared jeans, which spun me out a bit. Later on I was to discover that the northerners favoured the semi-flare and flare to show off their natty footwear.

Next game up was Pompey at home. After last season, we suspected the police would be on top from the off. We felt we had redeemed ourselves at Portsmouth last March after the hammering they dealt us at home and this time we expected them to be of the same calibre. I was in the city early that day for some reason and went back to Cardiff Central to meet the Neath train. I felt a tap on the shoulder and turned to face a lanky, skinny lad sporting an Aquascutum hat, scarf, tie and blazer. He spoke very softly.

"We're coming mate, big time."

I grinned and thought he was fronting me. Was he under-cover or what? I couldn't work it out. After a few exchanged words I realised that he was one of Pompey's main faces and started having a chat. He informed me that 200 were coming by service train and another 30 or so of his lot were drinking in town. I hit it off with him straight away – I always had respect for Pompey – and we talked about the previous season's events.

I had never met anyone like him before. He was absolutely obsessed with football violence, to the point of being a bit weird. I appreciated his honesty in telling me that he rated us for what we done in Portsmouth and I returned the compliment. He then suggested to me that we organise a private row away from the city centre between his 30 and a mob of the same numbers from Cardiff. Afterwards, he said, we could all go out for a meal together and chat about it. It was bizarre.

Next thing, a Portsmouth CID officer tapped him on the shoulder. "Raffles, You'd better keep out of trouble today.

I saw you knock that Zulu out on Wednesday night at Birmingham."

"Have you seen my nephew officer? He's going to be a proper little rower," proclaimed Raffles, taking a photograph out of his wallet and proudly showing it to the copper. This was the first time I had witnessed proper police surveillance on a suspect football hooligan. What with Raffles and the copper, I felt I was moving into a different league entirely.

Pompey's train turned in and I had another shock. Their entire firm were wearing Aquascutum blazers and Farah slacks. They had foxed the police in Portsmouth by saying they were going to a wedding in Bristol. I admired their cunning but was a little disappointed at the size of their turnout; it was a fraction of the mob from the previous season. After a few handshakes I raced back the Philharmonic to notify the boys.

We sat tight, knowing the police would have it sewn up outside Central station. I thought they would put Portsmouth in the Queen's Vault in Westgate Street but instead they decided to take them straight to the ground, and their mob was in there by mid-day. We were gutted and decided that the only way to have it with them would be to go in their end of the ground. Not surprisingly their mob were congregated in A Block of the Grandstand, so 80 of us paid to go into C Block and then walked underneath the main stand across to their section. We sent two spotters into mingle with them and give us updates of how well it was policed.

As we met up by the coffee bar under the Grandstand, Little Colin and Dai H said there were no Old Bill marshalling them, just a few of Cardiff City's stewards, as it had never been known to go off in the Grandstand, a section mainly occupied by "normal" fans. We waited for our opportunity and, as the teams came out onto the pitch, we sprinted up the staircase into their end. Pompey were shell-shocked and retracted to regroup and have a go at us. They seemed to be caught in two minds between steaming into us and panicking.

Dai H was first in. Pompey backed off and didn't trade any
blows. I noticed a lot of them were kids. They had mouthed
off at the station earlier, slagging us off for wearing tennis
gear, but now none of them were up for the row. They started
mouthing again when the police arrived and we were herded
in to the family enclosure. Cardiff's mob were given a heroes'
welcome by the Bob Bank as they were escorted around the
side of the pitch.

I recently discovered Raffles is no longer with us. He
committed a very sinister murder – according to an account
in the *News of the World*, he killed a gay man who had
propositioned him in London and wrote "6.57 Crew" in his
blood on the wall – and then killed himself in jail. He was one
of the nicest football lads I have ever met but was completely
wrapped up in the whole culture. He obviously also had
severe anti-social tendencies, which eventually caught up
with him.

The newspapers were horrified by the unprecedented
violence in the Grandstand that day and the *South Wales Echo*
ran a "name and shame" campaign to identify the culprits
from photographs. One of our lads was sussed and subsequently received a year's ban from the ground and a £300
fine. These days for the same offence he would have been
looking at bird, and any lad who is willing to fight inside a
ground is running a big risk. In fact CCTV cameras are
making it extremely difficult to have an off anywhere. Get
caught on film and you are bang to rights, and with the
current climate you would almost certainly be made an
example of, which would mean a custodial sentence.

Our next big venture was Chelsea away. They had a
reputation as one of only a handful of clubs to come to Ninian
Park and conquer. Cardiff, however, had fared better at
Stamford Bridge, especially when we took a massive mob in
'77 and smashed up their newly-erected scoreboard. Despite
that, a lot of so-called lads were missing at Stamford Bridge

that wet October afternoon. We ended up with a poor turnout of 80 on the train and another 50 or so by car. We were very well protected by the police all the way up on the train and escorted to the Tube for our journey to Fulham Broadway, where we were welcomed by a few Headhunters mooching about and some sly punches directed at out escort from shop doorways. Inside the ground we suffered the worst downpour of rain I have ever had the displeasure of standing in at a football match. I was soaked to the skin as we headed home. Chelsea did make a token effort to have a go at Paddington station. I remember seeing Icky and Giles, two of their leaders, gobbing off and swearing they would be at Ninian Park later on in the season to give us our annual beating from the Headhunters. Unfortunately for us they kept their promise.

By Christmas, the team predictably were struggling to keep up with the likes of Leeds, Chelsea and Man City. A trip to Sheffield Wednesday the Saturday before Yuletide didn't have much of an appeal to most of City's firm so a carload of us detoured on the way to Manchester to take advantage of the brilliant selection of clothes shops there, such as Hurleys, Gans-Gear and Shoebox, not forgetting the newly-opened JD Sports, housing some of the best rare Adidas footwear on the planet. I was quite flush with the money I had made from the Ireland trips and treated myself to a suede coat and a pair of Olympia Adidas trainers. Shoebox, a little unit in the Oasis centre, was one of the best places in the UK for trainers. Jacko had purchased the only pair of burgundy Trimm Trabb I had ever seen from there and the place was a Mecca for rare terrace footwear.

Our journey over the Pennines to Hillsborough was marred by the news breaking on the radio that the IRA had bombed Harrods in London, killing Christmas shoppers. We were dismayed that innocent people had to suffer for nothing and compared it to normal football fans getting caught up in a fracas – it's not on. We got to Sheffield and City were 4-0 down by half-time. It was soon 5-0 and we decided to make a move. We had spent about 20 minutes in the ground.

We played host to Swansea on Boxing Day. An 11am kick-off didn't give either side a chance to get their mob together. No open pubs and no public transport meant a non-starter as far as "the off" was concerned. The only consolation was a much-needed 3-2 victory against the old enemy. An ageing John Toshack netted for the Gypos. Their team were a shadow of the side that had marched up the league a few years before. How the mighty had fallen. Things felt good. We picked up three more valuable points at Derby the day after, with 60 of us breaking off and legging Derby down the street, making it a very happy Christmas.

NINETEEN EIGHTY-FOUR was to be a memorable year for me personally. It was musically by far the best year ever, with bands like The Smiths, Grandmaster Flash, the SOS band, New Order and the Pointer Sisters all making their way to my DJ box. On the football front, I was now at an obsessive stage. It dominated my life, and music was the only release I could get from the shenanigans on the terraces. I was not alone: the football hooligan culture had become a way of life for many by 1984.

The first Saturday in January, we played host to Ipswich Town in the FA Cup third round. They were no threat to our firm, so we decided to skip the match and go shopping for some January sale bargains. Whilst we were in town, Gareth pointed out a football lad, clad in Burberry scarf and sad Adidas trainers, who turned out to be one of Swansea's lads called Boxer. We confronted him, gave him a hard time and escorted him from the city centre to the railway station. But for a police presence we would have robbed him of his wallet and scarf. This was a bit of a naughty trick to play, seeing as he was on his own.

Barry Town were to visit Swansea in a Welsh Cup tie later

that month, so I tried to arrange with Boxer a row between the two sets of boys, but he seemed confused at what I was trying to plan. He obviously did not realise that Barry was one of Cardiff's strongholds. It is a rough little dockside town, ten miles outside Cardiff, with many council estates and one of the worst crime rates in the country. We knew all the Barry boys. They drank in a pub called the Windsor, which was nicknamed "the zoo", for obvious reasons.

On the night of the game, about 50 of us – 40 from Barry and ten from Neath – went to Swansea by train. We got off at High Street station and walked straight down to the Badminton, one of their boozers. No Jacks were there so we headed straight onto the North Bank, which was their end. We were very vocal and attracted the attention of about 20 of their lads. Karl, one of the most respected Cardiff lads ever, wandered over to them and started to arrange the off. We backed him up when Swansea started steaming into him on his own and flew straight into them. They were shocked. I went straight for Boxer, who now realised what my gestures had been about in Cardiff the previous Saturday.

Swansea document to all and sundry their "swim away" victory, when they chased a load of Port Talbot youngsters into the sea in a League Cup tie in the late '80s. But they have short memories and this one they choose conveniently to forget about. They had been told that Barry were bringing a mob and chose to disrespect it. We chased them across the North Bank. Barry Town have a reputation that Reading and Aberdeen will vouch for: Reading were drawn against the seasiders in 1984 in an FA Cup first-round tie and came unstuck at Jenner Park; Aberdeen likewise in 1996 also fell foul of this nasty little seaside resort, better known for its Butlin's Holiday Camp and the oil slick which ruined the coastline in the early '70s.

Pompey away was the next big one. In the previous season we had taken our biggest away firm for years but this time

took a fifth of that mob. We had settled a score or two at home
in September. We also had Leeds the following week, potentially
our biggest home game for years, so few of the lads wanted to
risk missing it by getting locked up at Portsmouth. The massive
police presence at Fratton Park that day quashed any opportunities for disorder anyway. Portsmouth were well turned out
both in the size of their mob and their sharp terrace style.
They'd had a pretty torrid time at home to Chelsea a couple of
weeks before, a bitter rivalry throughout the '80s, and were up
for revenge for their fiasco at Ninian Park in September.

Leeds United paid their first visit to Ninian Park in 12
years. The last time had been a 1972 FA Cup tie which
resulted in a 2-0 Leeds victory. That team consisted of the
likes of Johnny Giles, Alan Clark, Jackie Charlton and Billy
Bremner, to name just a few. I had watched the game on
Match of the Day at the tender age of seven. The 1984
equivalents were nowhere near the same calibre as that great
team; in fact Leeds were going through the worst period in
their history, on the pitch that is.

I recall going to Oldham in 1981 and seeing coachload
after coachload of Leeds fans heading to Swansea for a First
Division fixture. I couldn't believe to this day how many lads
we saw in the service station that day, many in yellow Leeds
away kits. I was equally impressed with Leeds at Arsenal in
the same year. I was in London visiting relatives and popped
into Highbury to have a look. For the entire 90 minutes,
Leeds and Arsenal battled it out on the Clock End. Leeds
were near the relegation zone and in danger of dropping out
of the old First Division but still managed to take 10,000 fans
to North London that day.

So on the morning of the game at Ninian Park we were full
of expectation when the first service train from Yorkshire
pulled into Cardiff Central. Leeds' firm are, as I've said,
known as the Service Crew and so a massive firm was expected
to start running amok in Cardiff that morning. We were

shocked to see only about 150 lads come off, shielded by the police. We had a huge mob out that day of up to 800 lads, the equivalent of what we had taken to Pompey last season. Massive police security and the small number of Leeds lads knocking about the city prevented any trouble before the game. The only incident was when a Bristol train came in with 60 or so Leeds boys from the West Country. They were attacked just outside the station and were legged back onto the platform, catching the next train back to Bristol. Leeds also came a cropper outside Asteys on Wood Street, where a vanload of their lads were attacked by all the Ely youngsters, fronted by Peter M. All the older Cardiff firm were jammed in the Philharmonic, Great Western Hotel and the Albert.

Inside the ground – where Leeds scraped a 1-0 victory – the hugely disappointed mob of Cardiff spotted 50 or so of Griff's mob, who kept themselves to themselves in the E block of the Grandstand. About 80 Cardiff, myself included, left the Bob Bank ten minutes before the end and headed over to confront them. They realised what we were up to and gave it the big one as we entered the lower section of the Grandstand. A huge roar went up as our mob, led by Bubble steamed into them. They retreated back into the seated area of the Grandstand. The Old Bill were quickly on it and battered us with their truncheons down the stairwell of the stand. A big kick-off with the police now occurred as hundreds of Cardiff's firm realised what was happening and came bouncing over from the Bob Bank to our aid.

In the meantime, the mob of Leeds in the Grandstand cunningly left via the Family Enclosure and made themselves heard as they entered Sloper Road. They ran a big mob of Cardiff down the road and for a while were in control but our mob of 80 or so followed behind them and attacked them from the back. The other Cardiff mob realised what was happening and stood, so Leeds were now surrounded. We could see the fear in their faces as Cardiff claimed victory. Leeds fans were running through gardens to escape. One particular Leeds boy with ginger hair, clad in a fetching Harris tweed blazer, turned white with fear as his jacket was ripped from his back. Another had his head smashed into the railings of the adjacent park on Sloper Road. It was one of the biggest hidings I have seen Cardiff hand out.

A year later Leeds turned up for a night game at Ninian and their firm did far better. They came with two coachloads of lads and chased a mob of Cardiff down Sloper Road, only to be rounded up by the Bill and swiftly put onto the Grange End. I can remember Leeds' lads were all wearing 24-inch bell bottom flairs and looked quite a picture legging 40 of us down the road.

In the spring of 1984, Gary and myself resumed the trips to Southern Ireland in the search of bargain designer wear. Alas, our entrepreneurial exploits were dashed by a steep deflation of the Irish punt, meaning our cheaper Lacoste was no longer a buyer's market. Disappointed we returned to Neath with the thought of our local derby clash with Swansea at the Vetch Field on Easter Saturday. We knew things were going to be lively down there because the police had left the kick-off to 3pm. On the other hand we were also aware there would be a massive police presence. To escape the police would be very difficult, so a few weeks before the game we carefully planned our route. It was decided that our mob of 80 or so lads would meet in Neath, leaving the rest of Cardiff's firm of 400 or so to have a run around in Swansea early doors, distracting any attention that might focus on us.

After a few beers in the Angel Tavern in Neath we caught a local service bus into Swansea quadrant shopping centre. The day was particularly hot and as the beer kicked in to good effect we were bang up for a rumble with our rivals. We left it as late as possible so we could get to Swansea just before kick-off. The Old Bill didn't bat an eyelid when we arrived, assuming that we were local Swansea lads. Instead of heading for the West Terrace, which housed the Cardiff contingent, we went onto the opposite East Terrace, occupied normally by Swansea family types. The plan was to be as incognito as possible through the game and to leave the ground ten minutes before the end to go onto the Swansea North Bank unnoticed.

A couple of months earlier, a few of the Neath boys, including Neath Punk, Fulman and myself, had gone to Chelsea v West Ham at Stamford Bridge. The ICF left the ground early, much to the amusement of the Chelsea mob, but their mood soon changed when the ICF invaded the Shed, legging Chelsea everywhere. Tottenham had also done it the week before Easter at Arsenal, with some success, so we thought that we would be one step ahead of the Jacks and our invincible mob of 80 or so lads would take the piss. We were in for quite a shock.

On the East Terrace, we found that Peter's young mob from Ely had had the same idea as us. The Swansea fans on that end weren't any of their faces. We now had about 120 and tensions were growing because Swansea had sussed out that we had a heavy presence in one of their sections and began to taunt us from the North Bank. Only a fence separated us and I made idle chitchat with Ivy, one of their main players and most respected lads to this day. Although the Jacks are one of our worst enemies and hatred between us is always at fever pitch, I have great respect for a lot of their faces and Ivy is one of the gamest lads I have seen in action. I have had a personal vendetta with Boxer for a number for years but my hat comes off to him also. I feel pretty guilty at trying to relieve him of his garments in 1984; I'm sure he will understand. This is not a name-and-shame exercise, just an acknowledgement that these are Jacks who fought the cause for their side. I will probably get slated by some Cardiff lads for this but I can only speak what I think.

By 3.10pm on that broiling Easter Saturday we were already two goals to the good and easing our way to an emphatic victory at the hands of our old enemy. Some of our lads chose to invade the pitch from the East Terrace to celebrate our second goal. Having each had a bellyful of cider we decided to join them. After accosting some of the Cardiff players in celebration we turned our attention to the North Bank and baited Swansea to join us on the pitch. They made a poor effort to get on. Two Cardiff lads – Neath Punk and Ginger from Pen Coed – even got onto their end and steamed into a few of the Jacks before making a hasty retreat (the Pen Coed firm were always there or thereabouts in the 1980s). G and a few of the Millbank lot were on the fence of the North Bank showboating in front of their seething mob. One-nil to our firm.

Chaos still reigned on the pitch as one of the Cardiff mob chose to punch Swansea centre-half Nigel Stevenson, which sparked an outcry from some of the Swansea team. It took five minutes for the police to restore order. Neath Punk was escorted around the side of the pitch by the police and still had time to take off his belt and swing it at a Swansea fan who was having a go at him from the North Bank. This brought the biggest cheer of the day from our mob.

Things were going according to plan, on and off the pitch. Swansea were seething at our exploits as we got rounded up and packed back onto the East Terrace, to cheers from the majority of the 3,500 Cardiff fans on the West Terrace. We were 2-0 up at half-time, the police had let us stay together and we were planning our next big one. Surely this would make national headlines and good exposure for our firm. It couldn't get any better.

But as soon as Dean Saunders got a goal back for Swansea, the day started falling apart. Within ten minutes we had surrendered our lead and Swansea, favourites for relegation, wormed their way ahead 3-2. Not happy with our team's effort we left the ground ten minutes before the end as planned and made our way to the entrance of the North Bank. Lots of families and normal Swansea supporters were scurrying in different directions, fleeing the inevitable after-match anarchy that sets these derby games alight. We had a wicked 100 lads outside their end who were all up for the off. As we got to the gates of the North Bank, a small mob of Swansea appeared. You could see the colour draw from their faces, which went as white as their beloved team's shirts. Neath Punk and Duller were first in and we legged these few lads back into the ground, catching a couple and smashing them.

All of a sudden a massive roar came from the North Bank, signalling the end of the game, and Swansea began to empty onto the street. Our mob of 100 ran straight into the masses throwing punches and kicks but to no avail. Our first ones in got battered and Derrem, one of Cardiff's finest lads to this day, was knocked unconscious. Myself, Duller and Mexxie managed to pick him up as we tried to fend of the blows and kicks raining in on us. We dragged him out and brought him around but it was now beyond a joke. Practically the whole North Bank had realised what was happening and Swansea's mob of at least 500 were now well up for it. We were on the back foot but stood our ground for as long as possible. We eventually legged it onto the Kingsway, regrouped and stood again but took another annihilation. This continued all the way to Swansea Central station. Swansea may harp on about the swim-away incident but this was their hooligans' finest hour. Yuan, one of my mates from Neath, took a pretty bad hammering and, to rub salt in the wound, he was struck on the head by a large stone as we entered the station.

It was one of the worst days of my life at the time. That and the day that Swansea got promoted to the First Division recur in my nightmares. I was pissed off for weeks after. In hindsight we did pretty well taking it to them and the 100 or so lads, you know who you are, did themselves proud. We probably got what we deserved for being cheeky. Never mind; as the saying goes, worst things happen at sea, or in that case, Swansea.

CHAPTER EIGHT

Zulu Dawn

BY THE START of the 1984-5 season, terrace fashion was steering away from tennis and golf wear to a smarter designer look, with labels like Giorgio Armani being high on the shopping list of most footy lads. The 24-inch, bell-bottom flairs were also making a comeback, favoured by clubs north of Birmingham.

After my summer holiday in Calella, Spain, my first game back into action with Gary was at Wolves away. We had a particularly good mob out that day, with numbers topping 400 as we left Cardiff Central. The feeling of *déjà vu* came over me when I picked up a Saturday morning paper at Neath station. We had to change trains at Birmingham New Street, so I scanned the fixture list on the inside back page and was unpleasantly surprised to see West Ham at Aston Villa. That meant we might well bump into the ICF, still the most feared mob in the country. We always seemed to land on West Ham at New Street. As if that wasn't bad enough, the ever-growing mob of Zulus, now Birmingham's top mob, had a residency at New Street on Saturday afternoons.

Still, I was quietly confident with the mob that we had that we could hold our own. Surprisingly New Street was quiet when we got there and without too much persuasion we headed straight for Wolverhampton. We knew they would have a good welcome committee for us and this was a potential game for fireworks, as we had not played them for eight years.

Their previous visit to Ninian Park resulted in a lot of Wolves's boys being hospitalised after being attacked at the old Cardiff City Supporters' Club clubhouse behind the Canton Stand in 1976. They did have a firm called the Subway Army and stories coming from some lads in Cardiff who followed other teams suggested that this could be a difficult trip.

I travelled with Julian and John from Porth and Rawlins from Cwmbran, three of Cardiff's main players. Rawlins was fresh from his spell in the armed services and could look after himself, so I was in good company. He is still active at matches despite suffering a severe knife wound in Blackpool in the late '80s that nearly killed him. Our train arrived in Wolverhampton at about 11am and Wolves were waiting for us in a pub across the road. We managed to force them back into the pub before the police arrived.

This proved to be the start of a long feud between Cardiff and Wolves in the 1980s. Their demise as a team in that decade – they were caught on a downward slope that took them from the top flight to the old Fourth Division and but for the goal-scoring genius of Steve Bull they might have stayed there – was a shock. Only 20 years previously they had been one of the best sides in Europe after turning over Honved of Hungary, considered to be the best club team in the world at the time. This must have been a bitter pill to swallow for the Molyneaux faithful and their fantastically loyal support. Indeed, in the 1988 fixture between us we managed to beat them 4-1, which was remarkable for Cardiff.

It went ballistic after the game as Wolves attacked our escort. A few of them tried to infiltrate our ranks and Dai H managed to hijack one of them and bring him back onto the train, where he was relieved of all his casual clothing and credit cards. About 50 of us managed to slip the escort and waited in Wolverhampton in a boozer across the road from the station. One of their lads, Growcott, was first into us as we went toe-to-toe with them in the high street. I had met

Growcott in Callela only weeks before and formed a good friendship, and he would be "guest of honour" at the Cardiff v Birmingham game just a few weeks later.

We got back onto Wolverhampton railway station with the thought of bumping into the ICF at New Street when a few Wolves tried braving it once again. They were well turned out, a few of them donning Luhta ski coats. I managed to have a one-on-one with one of their firm and knocked him to the ground with one of the best punches I have ever thrown. He was sporting an Adidas New Yorker sweat top. We got split up by a few Cardiff who told us the police were on our case, so I legged it off the station onto the tracks to avoid arrest.

The action was not over. When we eventually got back to New Street we were greeted by a full presence of ICF: about 150 of them, average age 30-plus, including Taff, who was one of the youngest. They were headed by the infamous Bill Gardiner, a legend even then. He and his intimidating lieutenants looked like they had just stepped out of a cell block at Alcatraz.

Gardiner was not impressed by our mob in the slightest. 'Get your fucking Toy Town firm off the platform,' he snarled. 'We're waiting for the Zulus and we don't need you spoiling it for us. We'll give you five minutes to fuck off.' Fortunately, because of my connections with Taff they left us alone, and we escaped a hiding from what I considered the best mob of lads that ever participated in the round-ball row. I felt a bit insulted by Gardiner's comments but Taffy said they had a score to settle with Birmingham after a few Cockneys had been cut the year before returning from a night game in Stoke.

We had a few games with Midlands teams that year, including Birmingham themselves. The Zulus had adopted their name through the size of their black contingent. In the late '70s Birmingham were known as a right-wing club but in

1983 black lads started joining their mob and by 1984 were
ruling the roost. They came to Ninian Park on a cold
December Saturday afternoon. A few of us decided to have a
pre-Christmas night out in Cardiff on the Friday before the
game and made plans to stay with Nick and Dai H. The latter
is one of the all-time legends of the Cardiff terraces and one
of my closest friends. We got togged up in our Lacoste shirts,
Farah slacks and mock-croc shoes and headed for the new
club in town called Caesars, which was owned by a regular
down at Ninian Park and where a lot of good lads were
employed, including Little Colin, a pocket-sized legend who
is the gamest lad I have ever seen at football: picture the
scene, a five-foot-nothing bar manager wanting to beat up all
his staff in the club for spilling a few of the punters' beers. On
the lighting rig, Chrissy Beer was in control. He too was one
of Cardiff's main lads in the early 1980s. It was a very plush
club based on the Camden Palace concept and was my first
real introduction to what would later take over my world. We
had a ball that night and I think everyone pulled, which made
it even better.

After one of Dai H's infamous cooked breakfasts we set off
nice and early to the Philharmonic. This was Cardiff's main
watering hole at the time and the attraction of 50p-a-pint for
cider or lager was too much to resist. Surprisingly they had
decided to extend their weekly 6pm-8pm happy hour to
include Saturdays and this soon caught on amongst the terrace
dandies. After every home game a mob of Soul Crew would
arrive, frequently drinking the bar dry.

Birmingham were late in that day and their train escort was
led straight to Ninian Park, a huge disappointment to the 400
lads we had out that day. The Philharmonic and the Royal
Hotel were jammed solid with lads. We did not rule out that
that the well-organised Zulu mob might spring a crafty one,
but nothing happened until we got to the ground. We marched
down through Canton, a suburb of Cardiff close to the ground,

and met up with the King's Castle mob. We now had over 600 worming their way through the side streets, avoiding any contact with the Old Bill. This was our biggest mob at home since Millwall two years before.

Nothing seemed to happen until we got to the crossroads on Sloper Road. Then a City Circular bus stopped adjacent to the crossroads and a mob of 80 or so came bombing down the road. It was difficult to identify them because it was very foggy. We presumed it was a mob of Cardiff because they got off a service bus, but suddenly a low, deep roar of, "Zulu, Zulu," went out. We were startled and at first backed off, not knowing how many of them there were. We soon regrouped and went into them but they stood and battle commenced. Another mob of Birmingham came through the park and the police had to let the dogs off their leads to hold them back.

The usual suspects immediately flew in. I tore my new Burberry jacket after throwing a rabbit punch which completely missed the Birmingham fan I had intentions of felling. I was then punched by a Frank Bruno lookalike. The next thing I knew I was being helped up from the floor, with birds twittering around my head like a *Tom and Jerry* cartoon. I was slightly concussed but the adrenaline got me going again. The fighting continued all the way up Sloper Road and eventually stopped outside the away terrace, the Grange End. Once the police had separated the two sides we got a chance to have a good look at them. The Zulus were well turned out in a nice selection of ski coats and suede and leather jackets. Ninety per cent of their firm were sporting 24-inch bell-bottoms with Gazelle, Munchen and Trimm Trabb being the choice of footwear. I also saw my first pair of green Trimm Trabb on one of the Brummies that day. I filed away a few fashion notes for later.

Birmingham won 2-1. After the match, everything seemed low-key as we worked our way back into the Philharmonic, where conversation inevitably centred on the pre-match confrontation. A few of the lads dispersed after the happy hour ended and by nine o'clock there were 60 of us left, mostly the West Glamorgan contingent waiting for the 10pm train home. All of a sudden one of the boys ran panic-stricken through the doors and informed us that a mob of Zulus were waiting in the alleyway behind the Philharmonic. He was covered head to toe in blood from a severe beating. We got tooled up and went in search for the Zulus, confident of a result with the good mob we had. Little did we know what awaited us.

We were immediately met by about 25 Zulus wielding blades. They just kept coming at us like robots. All you could see was the whites of their teeth, smiling at us. The row lasted for about five minutes – which is a long time – as we were scattered, then tried to regroup and have another go. I was hit on the head by a golfing umbrella and was out of action for the second time that day, and in the end Cardiff got annihilated, with Gary and a few of the Neath lot being chased up Caroline Street (or Salmonella Street as its known in these parts for the number of greasy chip shops that it houses). Fulman from Neath was the only one to stand and was saved by the police, who were quick to turn up.

Sometimes, if every football lad is honest, you breathe a heavy sigh of relief when the police save the day. In the 15-odd years that I was involved, this was by far the worst hammering we ever took. A few Cardiff got cut that night and those who were there are still haunted by the memory. I remember thinking at the time, *what I am doing in this game?* To this day I rate Birmingham in my top five hooligan mobs of all time, not just for the numbers but for their honesty and their appraisal of other firms.

CHAPTER NINE

The Famous CFC

MY FIRST MEMORIES of Chelsea – the famous CFC – were in 1977 at Ninian Park. By all accounts Cardiff had had a good go at the corresponding fixture at Stamford Bridge earlier on in the season, with 4,000 City fans smashing up their newly-installed scoreboard, much to the chagrin of the Londoners. Cardiff have a demolition mob, similar to Leeds, who just love disassembling metal objects but the boys in the firm see this as pointless.

I did not realise that day in 1977 that Chelsea would be up for revenge. They brought nearly 5,000 fans and I would say a third were up for a row, It was my first real taste of trouble. My father and I braved the walk down Sloper Road but met a mob of Chelsea who had just left the Craddock Hotel, on Tudor Road, and were hell-bent on ripping Cardiff's firm apart. They proceeded to go on the rampage, smashing up anything and anyone in their sight. My father took me to one side and sought refuge by knocking on an old lady's door. She was very understanding and let us into her home while the mob ran past.

Although very frightened, I was fascinated by the mayhem. I knew that one day I would want to be involved with the running mob. Fighting inside the enclosure that day drew most of my attention away from a 3-1 Chelsea victory. On the Monday after school, I ran to the newsagents to read the reports in the *South Wales Echo*; something I would do

repeatedly that season after trouble at Cup ties against
Tottenham Hotspur, Everton and Wrexham.

Two years later, Icky's coach were mad enough to come
onto the Bob Bank and took a real hiding in the corner near
the Grange End. Icky, or Steven Hickmott, was a charismatic
figure who later became nationally famous through the
Operation Own Goal hooligan prosecutions in London, when
he was at first jailed but then released when the convictions
were deemed unsafe. In the away end the rest of the Chelsea
mob fought with the police to try to rescue their firm but a
cordon of Old Bill and a 20-foot fence kept them back. On the
Monday after that game I recall Gorey from Neath being
spotted by his father on the television programme *Wales
Today* launching a Chelsea fan off the top of a wall separating
the Bob Bank and the Grange End.

The two big offs at Ninian Park with Chelsea in the '80s
were in September 1982 and March 1984. The first was a
landslide for Chelsea, who brought over 500 lads. A relatively
small turnout of Cardiff made the job easy for the Cockneys.
I remember ripping a brand new pair of Lois cords whilst
retreating from a mob of 80 or so who chased 20 of us
through Cardiff bus station. It was very much that kind of day
as probably the most feared mob to come to Cardiff in that
decade preyed on our firm.

Our biggest game of the 83-84 season was Chelsea at
home. The boys from the Bridge were sailing away with the
Second Division championship and we were looking shaky
for a swift return to Division Three. A win for us was
imperative while victory for Chelsea would more or less
guarantee promotion. Our mob had improved ten-fold on
two years ago and we were well up for revenge. In those days
for a big home game we would always muster up a mob of 25
or so from Neath and over 50 from the Pure Violence Mob
(PVM) from Port Talbot. Port Talbot is one of the toughest
little towns anywhere and its Sandfields estate is officially one

of the roughest in Europe. It relies on the neighbouring steelworks for employment. Port Talbot lads always outnumbered the Neath boys and local rivalry was strong but was put aside on match days, and a unit from West Glamorgan was always there. The PVM regularly went to Swansea nightclubbing and getting into rucks with their firm. Likewise Swansea would come mob-handed to Neath and Port Talbot. By the mid-80s, things got personal between Swansea and the West Glamorgan Blues, resulting in many visits by both mobs to well-known lads' houses. Swansea would even abuse known faces' mothers and fathers on the phone.

There was a massive police presence at Cardiff station for the Chelsea game. We knew they were coming by train so we retreated to the Tudor pub where we knew Cardiff would be drinking. As we left the station we clocked a mob of 30 or so Cockneys decked out in Aquascutum and Burberry. We chased them through Riverside, a rough suburb of Cardiff with many alleyways. This put the frighteners on them and they split into several factions. We caught ten of them and two ended up in the River Taff, while the rest lost their tennis wear and jewellery. We found out later that they were from Bristol and Hereford and had arrived early in Cardiff to accompany a massive mob of Cockneys due in minutes later. Trouble already and it was only ten o'clock in the morning.

We mobbed up in the Tudor and by 11.30 we had over 300 boys, including all the main faces. Bang on time the London to Swansea train arrived in Cardiff Central. We presumed that the massive police presence would escort them straight to the ground. We sent a couple of younger boys to spot their mob. Right on queue some of the Llanishen and Llanedden boys reported back that over 500 Chelsea were being held by the police in Cardiff Central. But a major breakdown in communication by the OB resulted in 200 Chelsea slipping the escort and making their way down Tudor Road towards our boozer. Their firm were no strangers to these parts and knew exactly the route to find us. The recent history of the two clubs added spice to the unnerving atmosphere and butterflies were fluttering around in my belly. We knew that this would be our ultimate test.

We all plucked up courage and ran out of the boozer to the on-coming Chelsea mob. They were raging and sprinted towards us, backing us off initially. We regrouped and stood toe-to-toe in the middle of the road with their firm. We did well, trading blows with the Cockneys in a wild melee of fists and feet. The Old Bill were quick to intervene and split the two mobs to either side of the road. Honours so far were even and Chelsea knew they were in for a battle.

The police closed down the Tudor and dispersed our firm in different directions. By midday we had over 500 lads out but split into three different mobs all over the city. With the 12 o'clock train bringing in another 400 Chelsea, our only option was to pick them off in groups. The mob of 150 I was with headed towards Canton to one of our favourite hideouts, the King's Castle, where a lot of main faces drank. The Cockneys arriving by cars and vans were by now having a hard time; as they arrived near the ground many of their vehicles were smashed up outside the Ninian Park pub. Police sirens would be heard all day as splinter groups of Chelsea landed on mobs of Cardiff.

Inside the ground there was a crowd of 11,000. Well over 7,000 of them were Chelsea. They filled the Grange End, Canton Stand, two enclosures and blocks E and F of the Grandstand, where the majority of Icky's firm were housed. The only part of the ground Cardiff had was the Bob Bank and a few lads in the Grandstand. We were in awe of the away following, recalling memories of when Sunderland came to Cardiff in 1980 with over 13,000 fans to celebrate promotion. Just after kick-off an almighty roar went up on the Bob Bank. About 20 or so cheeky Cockneys tried it on but we smashed them all over the terracing. Chelsea were tooled up but a few of one of our main firm disarmed them and some needed hospital treatment after ammonia was thrown in their eyes. At the time things were getting a bit heavy between football firms and blades were very popular as well as ammonia and Olbas oil disguised in Jif lemon bottles. Bleach was also used to ruin designer clothing.

Amazingly, on the pitch we were 3-0 up after 25 minutes and looking odds-on to survive another relegation dogfight, but even the on-field excitement was overshadowed by the antics in the Grandstand, where most of Chelsea's main faces were giving Cardiff loads of grief.

Things were getting tense as we hung onto our lead with only ten minutes to play. We clocked Chelsea's firm from the Grandstand leaving ten minutes before the end, obviously disgruntled by their team's performance. We sussed their next move would be to probably come on the Bob Bank, so we moved to the exit to await them. Right on cue, 200 Chelsea walked towards us behind the Canton Stand. We felt we'd had the upper hand before the game and there was no way Chelsea were going to take the Bob Bank now. We fought like demons to defend it and chased Chelsea back towards the Supporters' Club shop. In the end Chelsea were fighting amongst themselves to escape the mob of Taffies.

In the confusion we heard two massive roars from within the ground. The police regained control and pushed us back on to the Bob Bank, where we learned that Chelsea had scored twice within a minute to make it 3-2. Incredibly, they then completed a remarkable comeback by equalising right at the death. This sparked fury on the Bob Bank. Incensed by the equaliser and the thought of Chelsea taking the piss outside, we mobbed up and made a move to get Icky's firm from the Grandstand. A lot of Chelsea are similar to Cardiff, they don't know who is who amongst their large firm. Also, a lot of their fans that wear team shirts will have a go as well as their "boys". So when we confronted them outside, to my surprise the lads in the team kits were the ones keenest to get into us. We did well for a while and legged a few Chelsea into the park next to the ground, but as more and more Head-hunters poured out we were swamped by their firm. Icky's mob moved into the park and invited us in there for some sport. Due to his firm's reputation, a lot of Cardiff bottled it.

We made our way back to the Ninian Park pub to regroup. The police were now panicking because there were over 700 Cardiff lads out and threw a blanket of uniforms across the road to try to separate the mobs. Both firms were determined to get at each other, and started fighting with the police. This was by far the worst trouble I had ever seen at Ninian Park and one of the most intimidating incidents I have ever been involved in. You just didn't know who was who. Chelsea's was also by far the best firm ever to come to Ninian, matched only by the Wales v England turnout in 1982 before the Spain World Cup.

We decided to try to attack the main bulk of Chelsea's train escort from the many side streets *en route*. The walk from Ninian to Central station could have been designed for this and many away fans have come a cropper. Not this day though. We steamed into a mob of Chelsea from one side street but sheer numbers forced us back. All colour was drained from my cheeks when a six-foot beast came lunging towards me with a butcher's knife. I ran for my life as he chased me down a side street. My only way of escape was to hurdle a ten-foot wall and I put Daley Thompson to shame with my effort, landing on the other side on top of a battered old Maxi Coupe in a carbon copy of David Soul's leap in *Starsky and Hutch*. As I breathed a huge sigh of relief, Gethin from London and Brian Brain from Neath hurdled the same wall. We fell about laughing at what we had just encountered. We were young lads and had done our best.

The fighting wasn't over that day by any stretch of the imagination. After a few pints in town we headed back towards the station to go home to Neath. About ten of us fought a pitched battle in the bus station with ten of their faces. I lost one of my Adidas Munchen trainers, much to the amusement of the boys on the home journey. We played Chelsea again in 1986, when we were in the Fourth Division, and upset the odds by pulling off a 2-1 League Cup win thanks to a Nicky Plataneur winner. We have not played them since (at the time of writing). Though I have long been inactive on the footie front I do maintain an interest and reckon that if the two mobs met these days the odds would be now fairly even. Most of our mob who fought in that big off in '84 still grace the Ninian Park terraces, while there is no doubt that Chelsea command maximum respect from the majority of Cardiff's firm and were the only team to ever regularly haunt us at home during the '70s and '80s. A lot of Cardiff's firm who travel to Thailand, especially Dai H, have formed friendships with some Chelsea who run bars over there. West Ham in the '80s were probably the governors but Chelsea were not far behind.

CHAPTER TEN

Satellite Wars

BY THE MID 1980s our neighbours Newport County started getting a little firm together. They had been whipping boys, offering little or no opposition in rowing circles, but by 1987 would turn up unannounced in Cardiff city centre on a Saturday afternoon for a row. This puzzled a lot of Cardiff and also began to seriously annoy them, to the extent that over the next few years we were constantly battling with our neighbours and by 1988 they were our biggest rivals.

Newport had always been a rough-arsed little satellite town, an overspill of Bristol and Cardiff. It is made up of many bleak council estates and has received a lot of media attention for its high crime rate. At one time it was the least likely place in the country to find your motor still intact on your return. We had a certain affection for them. In the late 1970s Cardiff fans would cheer Newport's score at half-time if they were winning and many of our lads felt sorry for their team, as they were always at the basement of the Football League. By the early '80s, things were changing, due to the demise of Cardiff's team and a sudden surge up Division Four by County, inspired by their pint-sized centre-forward Tommy Tynon. They were looking good for promotion.

The two teams met at the beginning of the 1980s in a Welsh Cup tie at Somerton Park and County produced a shock 2-0 victory. The half-time cheers for County scores soon turned to jeers, which grew louder as Newport produced an amazing feat the season after winning the Welsh Cup. This easy route into Europe for Welsh clubs gave them the opportunity to play some of the biggest teams on the Continent (in 1967 Cardiff had reached the semi-final of the European Cup Winners Cup, only to be knocked out by a last minute goal by SV Hamburg, and in 1972 we defeated the mighty Real Madrid at Ninian Park). Welsh clubs were renowned for falling at the first hurdle but in 1981 Newport, still in the Fourth Division, somehow reached the quarter-finals, only to lose to a disputed goal to East Germans Carl Zeiss Jena after gaining a highly creditable 2-2 draw in Berlin. At the time our bitter rivalry with Swansea had been renewed after a long absence and now we had County to contend with as well.

Newport duly gained promotion to Division Three, mean-ing we would face them in the league for the first time in many years. On Boxing Day, 1982, we beat them 3-2 at Ninian Park. Off the pitch was a non-event, with no County lads showing at all. The return fixture at Newport proved to be a promotion battle. We went up but they sadly just missed out, which proved to be the beginning of the end for the club. Things went quiet until 1985-86, by which time we were back in the football doldrums. We met them in a league fixture and took a good firm to Somerton Park expecting the usual walkover. Had we done our homework, we'd have known that among Newport's mob were many game lads who usually followed First Division clubs, only watching County games when big firms were in town. In fact in 1983 a few Portsmouth had come unstuck, one of them being stabbed in the stomach, whilst boarding their waiting bus home from County.

They turned out over 150 and were keen as mustard to get into us, which was a complete shock to our firm. We clashed on a busy crossroads. Jonsey from Canton was hurt quite badly and Dai H took a few belts. This startled us and the conversation on our 20-minute journey back to Cardiff was

not of the massacre we expected but of this new mob that
County had.

A few months later we were at home to Preston North End
and expected a big away mob from Lancashire with their
team in a promotion position. We duly turned out a substantial
welcome committee but were disappointed at Preston's
turnout. Eighty of us left the ground early to go for a drink.
One of our lads reported that 50 boys had been in the
Philharmonic and were making their way down Tudor Road
towards the ground. We of course presumed they were Preston
turning up late. But sometimes you put two and two together
and get five.

That day St Julian's, a Newport-based rugby union side,
were enjoying their big day in Cardiff as they had reached one
of the minor cup finals played at the Arms Park. This gave
Newport the excuse to bring a firm over to have a pop at
Cardiff. We met head-to-head with them by the Craddock
Pub on Tudor Road and they were well up for the row: so
much so that they fought us to a stalemate. They didn't run,
and that pissed us off.

Their brazen stroke of one-upmanship now had them
marked down as our main rivals. In the summer of '87 it
became common practice for Cardiff to turn up in Newport
town centre on a Saturday afternoon and kick it off, and *vice
versa*. Things came to a head one evening in a chip shop in
Newport, when one of our lads, Jerky, a stalwart on the
Cardiff terraces and another rare training shoe addict, cut up
one of County's lads, resulting in a spell at Her Majesty's
pleasure.

In May 1987, County reached the Welsh Cup final again
and were set to play Merthyr Tydfil at Ninian Park. Merthyr
is predominantly a mining community and boasts one of the
roughest council estates in the UK, the Gurnos. Due to its
high unemployment rate, Merthyr is also blighted by crime
and out-of-towners are rarely welcomed in the pubs or social

clubs of the surrounding valley. Cardiff has a massive firm from Merthyr and in the '70s bitter squabbles between factions from Llanrumney and Merthyr were often evident on the terraces.

On the morning of the final we mobbed up at the Philharmonic knowing County would be mob handed. We were 150-200 strong by 11am on a dull May Sunday. The usual spotters were sent to survey the opposition. Mobile phones, of the house brick size and weight, were just appearing, obviously a sign of the Thatcher years. Fashion was starting to change on the terraces as well. Woodies Emporium in Cardiff was booming and sales of Armani and Fiorucci and new brands like Naf-Naf and Stone Island were creeping onto the Bob Bank.

One of the youngsters came bombing back into the Philharmonic to inform us that Newport were 500-strong and were slapping anyone *en route* to the Philly. We took to the street and met head-to-head with County on the corner of St Mary's Street and Wood Street. County were untouchable that day and saw us off into Caroline Street. Myself and 20 other Cardiff retreated hastily into Mulligans Irish pub on the corner of Caroline Street. It was very much like the scene in Quadrophenia when the Rockers get chased by the Mods into a boozer on Brighton seafront. We managed to escape out of a side door of the pub, leaving bar staff screaming as County pelted all the windows through. The floor was a sea of glass.

We came out onto the side alley and met a mob of 30 or so Newport buzzing over their wrecking spree. We were livid by now and steamed into them, chasing them up the alleyway, Dai H bouncing a disused Tesco shopping trolley up and down on one poor lad's head. We were so wrapped up in legging them that we didn't realise the rest of Newport's mob had sussed the situation and begun the Charge of the Heavy Brigade towards us. We realised about 20 seconds before they got to us that we were in for the beating of our lives: a 400:20 ratio in their favour did not look too promising. We retreated – in fact I have never run so fast in my life. Any athletics coach would have been in awe of my sprinting, without the aid of any banned substances. As usual, Dai H had to go one better by standing to the end. In hindsight it was hysterical, the sight of him pushing his shopping trolley into the charging mob and then legging it.

The cocky bastards had got one over on us again. The only way to hit back, given their numerical superiority, was to pick them off. Carlton, Simon, Dai and myself cruised the streets to the ground in Carlton's Porsche 911. As we got near the stadium we spotted one of their main players, Lemmie, with four of his mates so we sprung out of the car and attacked them on the corner by the Ninian Park pub. I decked one of their boys and we chased the others up the road. This was a little bit of revenge for us: the five lads had all been show-boating in town earlier after they had run us.

It was to be our only personal result of the day. A couple of their boys encroached onto the Bob Bank, which was the neutral supporters' end that day, and were given their marching orders by the swelling mob of Cardiff, who had heard of our embarrassment earlier on. After the game we got into County by the Ninian Park pub again and it was fairly even. One of the County boys of West Indian origin was doused in fuel as he passed the petrol station and some Cardiff lads then started chucking matches at him. The hatred had obviously reached fever pitch, with Newport providing stiffer opposition than the Jacks.

The game had finished 2-2 and led to a replay at Ninian Park. County were a little disappointing the second time around. The only incident that night came just before the game started when 20 of us stood against 150 or so but they never stepped over the threshold to mix it up with us. This went a big step towards making amends for the Sunday disaster. The animosity between Newport and Cardiff these days has quelled and I have formed several good friendships with County boys. City did however play the now non-leaguers in a pre-season friendly more recently, resulting in a mob of 50 lads going over on a service bus, thus foxing the local constabulary. The 50 were escorted away from the ground and sat in a boozer, waiting for County to make a move. They turned up 70-handed and it went off toe-to-toe, despite a police presence. The respect earned by both mobs was shown when their escort was clapped into Newport railway station that night by County's mob, and Cardiff returned the compliment, much to the bemusement of the police.

CHAPTER ELEVEN

Pump Up The Volume

MY FIRST MEETING with the co-author of this book, Anthony, was not on the terraces at some rain-drenched Third Division ground but in the salubrious surrounds of the Arches nightspot in Neath. I was promoting and DJ-ing at a Thursday night acid house kind of party, in 1988. We recognised each other from our terrace antics. Tony looked like a cowboy, decked out in the latest ultimately forgettable clubwear of Mexican poncho and bright-coloured kickers with 12-inch Simpson flares. Robert Barker, a local clothes retailer, always had his finger on the pulse for terrace chic and had obviously cashed in with the baggy look that bands like the Stone Roses, Charlatans and Happy Mondays were adopting. He was the first retailer to stock Lacoste in Wales, starting out in his hometown of Blackwood, a little Rumney Valley town better known for producing the band the Manic Street Preachers. Blackwood was a hotbed of fashion right back to the Northern Soul days, when busloads of soulful Welsh folk would trek up-north to the Wigan Casino and the Twisted Wheel. Steve Strange, who had a big hit with "Fade to Grey" with Visage, was among this elite and a good friend of mine, another Tony, who runs a small retail clothing outlet in Blackwood called Route, organised the trips. He had me entranced with some of his stories about Northern Soul and football matches in the early '70s and he, Robert Barker and my good friend

John Harris, one of Man U's old firm, remain my clothing mentors.

By 1988 a shift from the terraces to the dance floor was becoming apparent. Clubs like the Hacienda, Konspiracy and the Boardwalk in Manchester, Quadrant Park in Liverpool and the big warehouse parties of Sunrise and Biology in London were becoming the weekend buzz as the dwindling mobs of footie boys became fed up of punching each other. I was hooked on infectious 4-4 House grooves and soon acquired a pair of turntables and a mixer. To add to my many disco 12-inch singles, I was buying new dance music sounds originating in New York and Chicago.

Soon I was DJ-ing in Neath alongside Dai H, who co-promoted the night with me. We ran a successful Thursday night alternative to the Stock, Aitken and Waterman cheesy sound that was around in the late '80s. The new sound hit the scene like a hurricane and the whole way of clubbing changed. I was to spend many nights popping pills on the Hacienda's dancefloor with my mate Wigan and a host of lads who supported Man Utd, Liverpool, Blackburn, Man City and so on. All these hooligans danced under one roof on the happy tablets. I doubt you will ever get that situation again.

Nineteen eighty-nine saw a big reduction in football-related offences. The police thought they had kicked it and the Government was crowing, not realizing that the lads from the terraces were turning their hands to making money by dealing Ecstasy, DJ-ing, promoting and running dance music labels as well as having a wicked time with people on the same buzz. Fashion models stood next to footie hooligans on the dance floor and shared a good time. What other chance would you ever have to do that?

I progressed as a DJ and eventually met my current business partner and best mate Craig Barlett, a veteran of the terraces himself with both Cardiff City and West Ham. It was obvious we would end up running nights together because we thought the same, both musically and clothes-wise, and shared a passion for Cardiff City. I bumped into Craig at concerts like the Stone Roses at Spike Island and the Happy Mondays' famous gig at the G-Mex in Manchester, completely twatted on Es and trips. At Spike Island I asked him the simple question of how he got to the gig and he replied, "Three Es, two trips and a quarter of Black Moroccan." Say no more; it was that kind of day. On our journey home, Melvin, another ex-main player at Cardiff and a good friend of mine, was battered on strong LSD – like myself. He was asked to bring back some food and drink from a service station shop by his wife, who did not realize he was experiencing a higher state of consciousness. He came back to the coach bearing a pot noodle and a carton of undiluted Ribena. I don't think I have laughed so much.

Gradually my DJ-ing career took over from my antics on the terraces and Craig and I were soon promoting our own nights in Cardiff. After a two-year break to pursue our own ventures, we reformed in 1993 and co-promoted Spice of Life at Cardiff University. Soon the likes of Paul Oakenfold, Rocky and Diesel and Ashley Beadel all graced the hallowed turntables. The '90s became a bit of a blur as we experimented with all kinds of chemicals. By 1996 Craig had set up his own business called Woosh, a joint clothes and record shop. He specialized in labels that were more geared towards the glammy side of clubbing like Comme De Garcon, John Richmond, Nicole Fahri and Patrick Cox.

We were also gaining a reputation outside Cardiff and secured a residency at the Swansea Escape club. This, a few years previously, would have been unheard of, as I was Public Enemy Number One for a while with the Jacks. We managed to go unscathed for three happy years at one of the best clubs in Wales and, in fairness, bonded with the Swansea crowd. None of their boys frequented the club at the time except Owain, who I remain friendly with, although we did come to blows at a club night in Cardiff when he was MC-ing for a local hard-core DJ, but have since put the football thing to one side. On match days it might be a different story but I'm sure we would both go out of our way to avoid a personal confrontation.

By 1998 we were DJ-ing in Germany, Switzerland, Denmark and, of course, Ibiza. I found that most of the people in the dance music fraternity had been connected to football violence. Every year, the dance music business holds a conference in Miami, Florida. As we laze by the poolside, the topic of conversation – helped along by the odd line of white powder – is not of the newest release but of the old days on the terraces, with 90 per cent of the talk geared towards how mad Cardiff City Soul Crew were! Not blowing our own trumpet but promoters and DJs who follow clubs like Chelsea, Spurs, Arsenal, Man United, Leeds, Pompey, Millwall and Hull City have all paid tribute to us. I always compare Cardiff's Soul Crew to England's hooligan support: a very big mob but no organisational skills and a lot of internal squabbling.

Over the past three years we have been promoting a night called Lamerica which specializes in American House and disco grooves. Our aim over the next few years is to open our own club. Many faces from the terraces have been seen cutting the rug at our nights and recently we picked up two gongs at the Welsh Dance Music Awards. I am quiet fortunate that it has sidetracked me away from the shenanigans of the football. With such attention being focused on the unruly element at Cardiff City over the past few years, I have too much to lose with both my family and my business. Over the past year or so there have been some severe bans dished out by the magistrates. With the rebirth of our sleeping giant under the guidance of extrovert Sam Hammam, better known for his days as Wimbledon chairman, the risk of getting banned from watching these days would be heart-breaking. For many years the off-the-field antics hit the front pages while dire performances on the pitch made the back pages for the wrong reasons. In those days it would have been deemed a polite backhander from the judge and a result for your solicitor if you were banned from Ninian Park.

The installation of CCTV has made the hooligan runaround like a game of chess between mobs and the police. The mobile phone era revolutionised communications, making it difficult for the police to track down the mobs. Yet at the same time Internet websites encouraging violence and highlighting the "British disease" have inadvertently provided a lot of police intelligence. Even though the buzz from dance music has decreased and many footie lads seem to be returning to their old ways, I shall not take the risk anymore.

I would, however, defend the lads, even though this may seem strange to most people. The media seem to put football thugs in the same bracket as terrorists and paedophiles. This is totally ridiculous. The majority of football boys are, believe it or not, decent lads with good jobs and families, out for a release from the day-to-day pressures of life. There are Cardiff lads who have run around with the Soul Crew while holding down jobs like solicitor and doctor and a couple are even linked to the club in some capacity. As singer/songwriter Paul Heaton of The Beautiful South (who wrote the foreword to the hooligan book *Blades Business Crew*) once said in an *NME* interview, "Football hooligans are the most loyal supporters. They travel the length and breadth of the land, braving all kinds of weather and endless traffic jams." Why? Because the buzz of kicking off at a match, seconds before conflict, cannot be beaten by recreational or hard drugs. The adrenaline rush is amazing; so strong, in fact, that the only way you can kick the habit is to stay away. Even the older lads agree that it never leaves the system. Some of my closest friends are football hooligans and will remain my mates for life but by the 1990s I was out of it. So it's over to Tony to take up the story.

SECOND HALF

TONY'S STORY

CHAPTER TWELVE

Small Steps

I GREW UP in the heart of the Welsh Valleys in a small, sleepy village called Mountain Ash. It is predominantly a rugby town. I tried to fit in, playing the sport at a school where the sports teachers were ex-rugby players and hated the round ball. Annoyingly, rugby union is brainwashed into the psyche of your average Welshman. I disliked it, and the fact that every time I tried to play it, I failed abysmally and frequently got injured.

Instead I caught the bug of football from an early age, firstly playing and then spectating. I was taken to my first Cardiff game at the age of eight by my wonderful family, who ever since have regretted it. My first memories were the size of the place and realising it was never more than half full. By the time I was 13, I was going to matches with some local lads who were 16 and 17. I would have been forbidden to go just with them, unaccompanied by an adult, so I had to lie through my back teeth, with whoppers such as, "Oh, Alan Lewis's father is taking the car to Cardiff. Can I go mam, please, please?" She gave in every time. The times, though, I would phone home after a game, stuck waiting for the bus, saying, "Oh, the car's broken down. They're fixing it now. I will be home as soon as I can." My family must have sussed after a while.

My biggest friend at school was a lad called Mark but he was more interested in playing, as he was a quality footballer.

I was a fair player by the time I was 15, with a superb left peg: that's what I deluded myself with, anyway. My shortlived career ended at 17 but my last game was something to be proud of: Wales Under-18s YMCA versus England at Stoke, and we stuffed them 5-1. Watching City became my substitute.

I was always in some sort of trouble at school and beyond. Out of school I hung around with a group of friends who were mostly Roman Catholics and went to Cardinal Newman School, near Cardiff. They all had the same tastes as me. We were all big Cardiff fans, all into fashion – we were sportswear crazy – and music. Our musical tastes were pretty diverse for our age. One minute we would be listening to The Jam or Madness, the next Hip Hop like Run DMC, Beastie Boys, Roxanne Shante and the cool Electro compilations, which got us involved in break-dancing. We competed in break-dancing competitions all over South Wales. We also did a charity dance for Children in Need, after which they held an evening in the local youth club to thank us.

Football and clothes were my main passion though. At 14, I started to notice the older boys in the corner of the Bob Bank at City. They were all dressed in this way I hadn't seen before. Marco, a friend who was slightly older than me, informed me that these were called "dressers" and that they were part of "the Soul Crew". He knew some of the cooler dressers from school and told me that they were hanging up their tracksuits and spending huge amounts on this look. This was my first sight of the casual scene, at 14, and it stuck.

Marco took me to Newman School and I spent the day chatting to boys such as Sherbet, who is one of the best and became a very close mate of mine over the years. He was a Rhondda lad and a huge Cardiff fan. They would go on about the Soul Crew and the Under-Fives, a younger gang who were around our age and who followed Cardiff all over. Looking back, it was funny going into the hairdressers in Penrhiwceiber called Den Nolan's and asking for a wedge cut, like a New Romantics quiff but not so severe. Thank God I missed the early to mid-80s: horrific hairstyles some of them were – imagine wearing a quiff with a back perm? I remember people having really horrendous cuts. Mind you this is from a former body popper with a flat-top. Not the most flattering, ay?

The clothes for me swung from old school Adidas Long Beach tracksuits to Ellesse, Lacoste and Tacchini. The last three labels were usually out of reach, as pocket money rarely stretched to a £140 tracksuit, but I did acquire one or two. Labels for the young dresser who followed Cardiff then were Ralph Lauren, Emporio Armani, Classic Nouveau, Fiorucci, Chipie and C-17. Nowadays my favourites are Prada, CP Company and Mandarina Duck, which are very understated and, of course, extremely expensive. For most lads before their mid-twenties, fashion is very important, and when finances are limited it's hard to keep up with what you want. As you get older you like to dress down a bit more; you also have a bit more money and can afford the look you want, so style replaces fashion. The more-established labels became high street tat during the '90s, with every man and his dog getting access to them. Armani was really the only one that stood the test of time for coolness.

In those days only one exclusive store in Cardiff sold the stuff: Woodies. The boys went on about it so much I thought you needed an invitation just to get in the door. I finally turned up there after weeks of saving. I had been told about the prices beforehand but it was still a shock when I saw them for myself. *Fuck me*, I thought, *that jumper is £180, and £20 for a pair of socks!* My first purchase was a Ralph Lauren polo in navy blue, costing £32.50, closely followed by some jeans I got in the sale. When you're that age you love to show off and want everybody to see your label. The jeans didn't have anything on the pocket, just a Ralph Lauren leather badge for the belt to go under, but I made sure that badge was on, tucking in my top at every opportunity. I also carried that first Woodies bag for weeks. They even had denim shirts with "I get my goodies from Woodies" on the back. That was an absolute must.

I continued buying Fiorucci or Classic Nouveau tee-shirts from there. They were usually too big but I still bought them anyway just for the label, looking like a clown, no doubt, and walking around the village thinking, *Yeah, look at me, I've got a tee-shirt on which came from Woodies*. No-one from Mountain Ash gave a monkey's though. Robert Barker was another popular store for Cardiff dressers whose budget didn't quite stretch to Woodies. The stories which haunted me were of these lads spending all this dough on these garments, then having them ripped at the football.

At the City the classier casuals stood out a mile. Emporio Armani was a range of Giorgio's clobber at the time which caught the eye and was popular with lots of Cardiff. One very noticeable lad was Stevie Millbank, a copper-haired, fiery character from the Ely estate, which I soon realised was home to many of Cardiff's personnel in the 1980s and still is today. Steve and I laugh now about this little upstart from the Valleys enquiring where he got his cloth from. "Mind your own business, you cheeky cunt," was his first reply. *Cheers*, I thought, but I didn't say anything.

I was in awe of the group he was among. He would often turn up with a black eye and even today you will see him occasionally with a fresh one. It wasn't that he couldn't handle himself – he's as tough as the next – but I'm sure he was fighting every day. We go back a long way now and whenever we meet he treats me like a younger brother. If you don't know him he seems a bit daunting but he's a true gent.

It wasn't long before I was totally obsessed with the football fashion – and from there it was a gradual journey to fighting. One point I want to make is that young men do not suddenly decide to become "football hooligans". They arrive there by a series of small steps rather than one big jump. First you go to the matches, then you begin to look up to and emulate the older lads, then you notice the gangs and the excitement they generate, then maybe you witness a few skirmishes with rival fans, then you start to hang around the fringes, wanting to be accepted, and gradually, over a period of perhaps years, you join in. I had seen violence at football a couple of times, notably Chelsea at Cardiff in 1984 when I was with my mother, of all people. We sat in the Grandstand as the two mobs fought hand-to-hand 20 feet away. Two years later I saw some Wolves in the Bob Bank getting well and truly clattered after they celebrated a goal. But August 1987 was my first hands-on, shall we say, experience.

It was Cardiff vs Swansea at Ninian Park a few weeks into a new season. The summer sale was on at Woodies and I arrived in town at midday with my mates Marco and Curry. We noticed the atmosphere seemed usually tense. Still, we headed to the store where I bought some C-17 dungarees (I know, *dungarees*, but I was only 15, give me a break). Out on the street, we felt like strangers as we walked along among groups of well-dressed lads with strange haircuts, short and spiky or with a parting and a severe shave on the back and sides, the *Shine on Harvey Moon* style (which started a new craze in Den Nolan's hairdressers).

"You Swansea?" we were asked about ten times from town to the ground. Walking up Tudor Road was frightening as fights broke out around us. We saw a Swansea fan get pushed through a shop window. We broke off and turned right up towards the Ninian pub. As we got close, a minibus pulled up outside. We froze and watched as these 15 or so Swansea piled out. The doors of the pub burst open and Cardiff charged into the Jacks. Most Swansea managed to get back in the bus but a few didn't. One mad Swansea lad who was on crutches stood swinging a crutch until he was pulled to safety and the bus sped off.

What next? we thought. We crossed over the road, past the burger van and walked towards the ground, past the Ninian train platform. A large group were on their way to the ground, so innocently we mingled with them. We failed to notice the police wandering by the side of us. We were pretty naive. A six-foot ginger bloke, aged 30 if he was a day, turned to us and said to his mate, "These fuckers ain't with us." We carried on, none the wiser, until seconds later: "Come on!" This moustachioed Rambo came flailing his arms and then butted Chris full in the face. I would have been scared if it wasn't for the sheer shock as these grown men took turns punching us. We broke free and pleaded with a copper to help us. We were pushed away. The headbutting Jack kept coming for us until the police managed to calm him down.

We made double time to the ground and got onto the Bob Bank terrace. As kick-off approached Cardiff's mob in the corner of the Bob Bank grew and grew. Swansea had a core following of around 800, being generous, and around 50 noticeable boys in the corner. The atmosphere was ugly. Missile flew back and forth and it was the first time I had heard songs like, "You're gonna get your fuckin' head kicked in," and, "You'll never reach the station." I learned these had been a standard part of the repertoire in the 1970s and they were sung that day with deep feeling.

Just after kick-off, one Cardiff fan had enough of the Jacks being there. He climbed the fence at the front of the Bob Bank, forced his way past a couple of stewards and started to gesticulate towards the Jacks. He was about 6ft 2in and of large build. The Jacks didn't really say much as he did his best to climb over into them, reaching the top of the fence before being dragged back by three coppers. Cue the mob in the Bob Bank trying to join him. Fighting broke out with some police and a couple of coppers got trapped in the corner of the Bob Bank as up to 100 Cardiff waded in. One poor copper suffered more than most. He got to his feet, head covered in blood, truncheon by now in overdrive. More police turned up and waded in for a couple of minutes. It was ferocious. The boys and I kept as quiet as mice all the way through the game. We were scared yet exhilarated.

Cardiff won the game 1-0 and the players were just as passionate as the fans. A true Jack if ever there was one called Joe Allon butted our captain, Terry Boyle, right in front of the referee. What was it about Jacks and headbutting that day? We left the ground speedily, not wanting to get caught up in any more aggro. On the way home I was glad on two accounts: we won the game and I saw some Jacks getting a tuning. I did wonder why grown men would violently attack three youngsters barely in their teens.

It was the start of a feverishly exciting period of my life. I arrived home that evening to see that the fighting had made national news. It would lead to the arrests of 11 Cardiff fans, who were subsequently charged with riot, the first and only time to my knowledge that any football fans had been charged with such an offence. During the subsequent trial, which dragged on for a year, some of the riot charges were dropped when the prosecution realised the near-impossibility of them standing up in court. Four Cardiff fans did go to jail, however, with sentences ranging from four years down to 12 months.

I have to say that the prospect of a criminal conviction did not deter me from taking those small steps towards joining the Soul Crew. I have since appeared in court on numerous occasions for football-related offences, as have many other Cardiff followers. Of course it's nothing to be proud of but I was never ashamed of it either. It was just part and parcel of being a football lad. It went with the territory, an occupational hazard if you will.

I WAS IN that transitional phase from starry-eyed soccer fan to terrace obsessive. One thing I did enjoy was seeing other teams and visiting different towns. Most clubs have people like myself who, if it's not possible to watch their own team for whatever reason, need their fix of football. Later this became hoolie-spotting as much as footie-watching.

I was always fond of Liverpool, probably because they were the first team I saw on television as a youngster. I was taken to watch Cardiff and Wales many times as a child but going to Anfield was an early ambition, and for my twelfth birthday I and other family members had been given the opportunity: Liverpool vs West Ham. My mother had really done the business and I still have the photos to prove what I was wearing: an *A-Team* jumper and tracksuit bottoms with matching Liverpool hat and scarf. A nice little ensemble, if I say so myself.

We got as far as Birmingham and I recall loads of teenage and older men boarding. Looking back it may have been the Zulus. I thought how odd they looked with their brightly coloured clothes and hairstyles. There I was in an *A-Team* jumper thinking how stupid these people looked. They must have had some fun as they were away at Man United and it was 1984, one of the most troublesome years ever in football. Had I been a few years older I would have been nosing to see how many ICF were in Liverpool, but at 12 the only things on my mind were my heroes, Ian Rush and Kenny Dalgish.

I remember it all vividly, arriving at Anfield for the first time. With football you either get the bug early or not at all. I got it early and it will never go away. Liverpool won 6-0, not a bad start for me. After that I was taken as often as we could make it. Apart from some Swansea vs Liverpool encounters, the first Liverpool away game I saw was at Highbury, where they lost 2-0 on Niall Quinn's debut. He and Champagne Charlie Nicholas scored the goals.

In the 1988-9 season we followed most of Liverpool's Cup run. With the semi-final against Forest due to be played at Hillsborough, four of us from the Cynon Valley couldn't get tickets because of the demand. Still, Billy, who did most of the driving, enquired about hiring a car, with a view to going there anyway and trying to get in. But as it was a Bank Holiday weekend the hire company was insistent that we took the car for the extra day as well, and we couldn't really afford it, so decided to give the game a miss. I'll never forget that Saturday afternoon: Billy and I in front of my television watching *Grandstand*. Cardiff were at Bury and, as I had been there the previous season, I hadn't bothered going.

News reports came in at around 3.05 of crowd trouble. We instantly thought of Forest and Liverpool battling in some part of the ground. If only it was that simple. Looking back, any ticketless fan would have done exactly the same as those outside the Leppings Lane end. If you haven't got a ticket you will do your utmost to see the game. Today questions remain unanswered but even for someone like me, not a regular at Anfield, it was a horrible period. I was lucky enough to get a ticket for the final against Everton. It was an emotionally-charged afternoon and a superb occasion in memory of the Liverpool fans who couldn't be there.

One game which stands head and shoulders above the rest is when Liverpool play Man U. The first time I saw them clash was in 1987 at Old Trafford. We were on the supporters' bus with Cardiff's Man U branch. The Mancs had loads of boys on the lookout for Scousers hanging around outside Lou Macari's chip shop on the Warwick Road. We were in the Stretford End and Liverpool took the lead. Very naively we asked the stewards if we could be escorted around to the Liverpool end, as we weren't United fans. No chance. But New Year's Day, 1989, was the first time I really witnessed the bitter hatred between these two great north-west rivals. The Liverpool end was awash with inflatable aeroplanes of all shapes and 90 per cent of their songs were to do with the Munich air disaster. The best United could come back with were inflatable skeletons and "Shankly 81" songs. At the time

Liverpool were the dominant force in English football. Now the pendulum has swung, but I suspect the hatred will always remain.

By this time, however, I was heavily involved in our own battles.

WHEN IT COMES to football violence, the hardcore followers of Birmingham City have been regarded as top ten material for a long time now. I first went there for a night game in 1989. I was just a novice but was cornered to go on one of the two coaches of the rogue element. I think half of the coloured in Cardiff Docks – otherwise known as Tiger Bay – turned up. If City come up against a big mob like Birmingham or Millwall we can rely on these people to turn out, and we really did have some bad lads on board. Most of the Docks prefer to make their cash on the weekend by whatever means possible, so football doesn't come really high on their list of priorities, as there is no money to be made in having a fight at a match.

We were heading to the Bullring in the centre of Brum. I used to hear stories, "Watch yourself in the Bullring," and wondered what it was, not realising it was a shopping area. We got there at 6pm and marched about. I was pretty nervous, even though I was with the naughtiest bunch I could have hoped for. We got into a pub near the ground, still with no sign of trouble. When we left to go to the ground it was pitch dark. There were hordes of Birmingham fans walking by the side of us but no-one said anything. My heart was pounding. As we approached the ground outside the home end, a large group of lads were queuing to get in. I just followed as Cardiff ran straight into them, punching and kicking anyone in their way. When these Brummies got over the initial shock, they started fighting back. It was even numbers until many of the Birmingham who had already gone into the large terrace began to flood back out. "Zulu, Zulu, Zulu," was chanted louder and louder. I don't know how many were trying to come back out at us but it was hundreds.

The police then arrived on the scene and surrounded us. We were marched around to the away end. This was years before St Andrews was rebuilt and Birmingham were to our left on a massive terrace. They sang, "You're going to get what Crystal Palace had," a reference to a recent violent incident that had been widely shown on national television. The Cardiff firm were pleased with what they had achieved but we all knew it would be Rorke's Drift revisited outside, with the Welsh once again having to stand against a massive number of Zulus.

We were kept in for ages. At one stage two coppers come over and said, "There are five hundred of them waiting for you." We ended up in an escort back to our coaches and 40 Cardiff, mainly top Ely, broke away and had it toe-to-toe with 100 Zulus. The police intervened but eight Cardiff got through and stood against this 100. I have since spoken to Birmingham and they were full of praise for this little crew. So you can imagine the impression they made on me.

WITHIN A COUPLE of years of running with the Soul Crew, I had picked up a few of police cautions. My first proper brush with the law, however, came at Bristol City away on February 10, 1990. Hundreds of Cardiff fans rioted at the end of the game, fighting with the police and destroying the turnstiles as the thin blue line desperately tried to keep them back from a few hundred Bristol City outside. The season before, the gates had given way and the locals were run ragged but this time they held, despite Cardiff louts on top of the turnstiles smashing them with their Timberlands. They ended up as rubble while the police came under non-stop fire, to the eerie chant of, "We are evil, we are evil," adopted from Millwall and sung by arguably 1,000 voices.

Calm followed the storm and we were all let out and

escorted back to Temple Meads train station. The police took it as an opportunity to drag out fans they assumed were part of the trouble, including yours truly. I even remember what I had on, a dark purple puffa body warmer, Armani woolly jumper, C-17 flares and grey leather kickers. Puffa jackets were very popular for a few winters back then. Name a game and a year and I will remember what was in and what I had on, down to my footwear. Many lads around the country are the same, quite obsessed, and I imagine will still be looking for that exclusive label or old-school trainer in their fifties and sixties.

The case against me was affray and criminal damage. I was not guilty all the way. The court hearings spread over 18 months, back and fro to Wurzleland almost every month until a two-week Crown Court trial was set for 12 of us. In the meantime, Stone Island had become the new label for boys in the know. It was years before the Bristol City lot got their hands on it. When I turned up with a Stone Island coat on, a few of the local firm were there and I could see they took an interest in it. They would have been in for a decent struggle: I have never been the toughest of people but I'd have the strength of ten men if they tried to prize away a £500 coat! My barrister said I could be looking at three years if found guilty but the evidence was so thin it was laughed out of court and we were acquitted after a week. A nice expenses cheque of £500 arrived months later from the court, just in time for Wales's trip to Nuremberg in the European Championship qualifiers of 1991, but that's another tale.

CHAPTER THIRTEEN

The Jacks

THE FIRST-ROUND draw for the FA Cup isn't usually greeted with much enthusiasm in football circles but when the names came out of the hat back in 1991, we couldn't have wished for more. Cardiff City were drawn away to South Wales rivals Swansea City. Phones were red hot with news of the draw.

At that time, Friday nights usually meant travelling to a rave club or two. We would be totally smashed the next day, on our way to watch Cardiff playing in some English backwater. There were serious comedowns going to places like Chesterfield, Scunthorpe and other equally depressing holes. How I managed it half the time I will never know. The early Ecstasy days I suppose dulled a lot of the football lads' usual violent activities but it would not get in the way of this one for us. I vowed to keep a clear head.

Swansea hate Cardiff with a passion I couldn't even begin to explain. The feeling is mutual but not as deep: they really do seem to despise us more than we despise them. Perhaps there is more to it than football, with Cardiff being named the official capital city of Wales in 1955 and Swansea feeling they had been relegated to the status of a second-class city, the poor relations of Wales. But the football also goes a long way to explaining it. During the early to mid-Eighties, there was not much opposition at the Vetch and Cardiff would regularly terrorise both the place and its people. As the decade wore on, however, the Jacks got a firm together.

The first time I visited the Vetch with Cardiff was in the Littlewoods Cup in 1988. Cardiff had lost the first leg 1-0 at home. For the return we had around 800 fans in one of the dingy pens behind the goal. I had just turned 16 and travelled with my mates from Mountain Ash, including Geraint. I didn't really know any of the boys but I knew who they were. We won the game 2-0 in extra time with goals from Terry Boyle and Paul Wheeler. When the second one went in it was sheer pandemonium in the away end, grown men with contorted faces screaming with delight. The Jacks to our left in the North Bank went mental trying to invade the pitch, fighting with both the stewards and the police in their bid to reach us. When the game finished, everyone dispersed. We got into the car park safely but going on around us were the usual battles that became common in that area opposite the prison.

Cardiff had a notorious bunch of lads from Port Talbot who called themselves the Pure Violence Mob (PVM). These headed for town led by a half-caste lad who was making a big name for himself. Forty PVM that night fought and held off over 100 Swansea: the police had to baton-charge the Port Talbot away from Swansea town centre and back on to the seafront. It calmed for a while so the Port Talbot lot began to disperse to their vans parked by the Guild Hall near Swansea Bay. A group of eight didn't get home safely. As they approached their van, a huge mob of Jacks came charging around the corner. Many of the Port Talbot lads were barely 18 and panicked. The Jacks scattered them from the seafront and some were chased into the sea. To this day the Jacks see this as some sort of major achievement and the "swim-away" story has been documented in different books and magazines. Even other teams, like Millwall and Wrexham, have sung about it to try to get a rise out of us (which worked).

Little outbreaks of violence occurred regularly at Cardiff-Swansea games but rarely did the two mobs come face-to-face with no police intervention. Many Cardiff boys believed that the Jacks could not live with them if it ever happened. Maybe Swansea felt the same way. The FA Cup draw in 1991 brought the game that would decide who were the governors of Wales. A full turnout of boys from both clubs was guaranteed.

By the time of the game I had forged good friendships with Cardiff lads from all over and been involved in many scraps with them. At the time the main lads came from the Docks (home of the fiercest fighters I've ever seen), Ely, Roath, Llantrisant, Barry and Neath, with a few from the Valleys like Porth in the Rhondda, Aberdare and Merthyr. Cardiff's catchment area covers the whole of Wales; probably every village and town in Wales is home to a Cardiff fan, or groups of. Most of the main faces arranged to meet up in a quiet pub in Neath at around 11.30am. Neath is a staunch Cardiff area, despite being only ten miles from Swansea. The chosen pub was perfect, away from the town centre and prying eyes.

I turned up with mates from Ebbw Vale, a game nutter called Nigel, Brynmawr and Merthyr. The pub was already full. Viking and John were there from the Docks with a good contingent of their crew; when these lads turn out, you know someone is in trouble. By noon there must have been 150 Cardiff in this pub and the beer was flowing – but not too much, because a job needed doing. Out loud I was confident that with such a mob we could take over Swansea, but in the back of my mind I knew that the Jacks would be heavy. They hardly travel anywhere but at home they can be a difficult proposition and of course this was the FA Cup and Cardiff at home was their final.

It was years before mobile phones would become common but we heard through the grapevine that the police in Swansea were forcing most of the pubs to shut early. It didn't take them long either to get wind of where we were and our cover was blown. The plan was to travel to the game in minibuses, as the trains and coaches would be heavily policed. Now the cops were on our case, it was decided that our minibuses would leave separately rather than in convoy and park near the leisure centre in Swansea. There must have been 20 of us crammed into the back of our vehicle. Outside, the rain was pelting down as we drove along the seafront. The driver dropped us off and made his way to park up.

Surprisingly there were no police about and it didn't take us long to hear it kicking off down the road. The 20 of us marched down past the prison and crossed to road, but it was the Jacks who found us straight away. "Come on then you Cardiff cunts" came a shout from behind us, as around 30 Swansea ran into the middle of the road. Game on. We steamed into them without hesitation. It looked like these Jacks had already been in the wars, with three or four covered in blood. It was a violent encounter and when two of them hit the deck the Swansea backed away. I recognised one of their lads. He was lucky to be there after Belgium away earlier in the year, but that's another story.

As we backed them off I cracked one of them over the head with my Burberry umbrella, breaking it as I did so. A few coppers turned up and managed to separate us. I screamed at one of the Jacks, "This is our day today, you're going to fucking get it today." As I said it, I got a truncheon right across the face, dropping me to my knees. As I staggered up to my feet there were fights all along the car park. More Cardiff had arrived and we now numbered up to 40, which included Matthew and Psycho, two of my closest pals, a couple of the Docks, Stanley of Llanishen, who was one of the gamest but is a pure gentleman, plus the two brothers from Ebbw Vale who were equally as mad and were seething looking for Swansea. Matthew put on a virtuoso display, pulling a cricket bat from underneath his three-quarter-length leather coat. He hit a couple of these Jacks for fours and sixes with Botham-like aplomb in possibly the best batting display in Swansea since Sir Garfield Sobers hit six sixes at St Helens, just down the road.

We broke away from the police and headed back towards the Jack pub to make our way into town. Another roar went up and a mob of around 100 Swansea came round the corner. We ran into them anyway, with only a few hesitating. A lot of these Jacks were much older that us and thankfully it was all over in seconds courtesy of our truncheon-wielding friends, who appeared from nowhere.

A couple of us sneaked off and walked into town. It was going off everywhere, sirens wailing all the time. Hundreds of Cardiff arriving by train were unbelievably being allowed to make their own way through the town centre without a police escort. It was crazy considering this was the first FA Cup meeting between the two teams in decades. I knew Cardiff had hundreds of boys but never before had I seen everyone in the same place. We joined a mob 300-strong and I couldn't get over the age of some of the men present. There was I, 19 years old in my new Stone Island coat thinking I was the boy, and these men were old enough to be my father. We had all shapes and sizes present, as a game like this brings everyone out of the woodwork and then some. Because Swansea's pubs were shut, their firm was all over the place, with little central organisation, and Cardiff were picking them off as we made our way to the ground.

As we approached the Vetch we charged towards the North Bank, where 150-200 Swansea men were waiting at the end of the road. They counter-charged, throwing bottles, glasses and stones. When the missiles stopped raining down we sprinted towards them and as soon as their ammunition ran out, they turned to flee. What a feeling. Running Swansea outside the North Bank was all my Christmases rolled into one. The chant of "Wales', Wales' number one" broke out as we chased them.

The police regained some sort of control and herded us into the ground. The Vetch was already full to the brim and the atmosphere was radioactive. Almost 3,000 Cardiff fans were squeezed in behind the goal, and a large percentage of them were clearly boys. Everyone at the game already had their own little stories. Some Bridgend had arrived early and the pub they were in, the King's Head, was attacked by a small amount of locals armed with bricks and bottles.

Just after kick-off, it went off in the stand to our right. Around 50 Cardiff had managed to get tickets in with the Jacks and there were fists and boots flying everywhere. As the fighting spilled onto the pitch, Keith Cooper, the referee blew up and took the players off. The Cardiff in the seats were the Neath lot, who had acquired tickets for where Swansea's mob usually sits. Some Jacks in the North Bank made a feeble effort to invade the pitch and a load of us screamed for them to get over as we too then tried to scale the fences, only to have our fingers cracked by truncheons. The police quelled everything and made a few arrests from the seats. The 50 or so Cardiff were then escorted around to our end where they received a hero's welcome. Swansea had never managed to sit in our seats at Ninian Park.

The game restarted and Cardiff began the better of the two teams, taking an early lead. This proved to be yet another false dawn on the pitch, with the Swans going on to beat us 2-1. After the final whistle we made our way to the seafront. There were double-decker buses laid on to take people directly to the train station but any lads were shouted at if they attempted to board them. Huge Cardiff lads in their 40s and many from the Docks were punching on the windows and yelling in thick Cardiff accents, "Get the fuck off the bus, we're walking." Most took heed. By the time we had made our way to the front, there must have been 400 Cardiff. The road was full.

Word soon spread: fuck the Old Bill and straight into town. We marched past the Jack pub and up towards the Quadrant with one police van tailing 400 boys. Past the Quadrant we chased a token 50 Swansea. I saw two or three Swansea fans I knew from Aberdare standing in the main bus stop. I smiled and waved and they waved back nervously. I made out they were Cardiff so they didn't get attacked: Cardiff's main boys do not bully but we have some idiots who think it's quite clever. I ain't one of them; there are rules to the hooligan game. We roamed the streets searching for the Jacks but without success. Some lads got bored looking and turned their attention to a jeweller's shop window and the Rolex watches on the other side of the glass, but they had no luck either.

We spotted a mob at the top of one of the main shopping streets and started to walk quickly towards them. There were hundreds of them coming towards us and it was all set for World War Three. As the roars went up I managed to get to the front and could see some of their faces. The first one belonged to a pure headcase I know from Aberdare called Sparky. But the thing was he was Cardiff – they were all Cardiff. We were stunned: as far as the eye could see stood this Cardiff mob. There must have been 800 of us in this street, maybe even 1,000. How can you estimate numbers in a mob this big? It was an army.

They were lads who had been on buses and who, halfway through their journey, had decided they wanted to stay. At some traffic lights they kicked the doors open, smashed the windows and made their way into town. This was the biggest mob I had ever seen. For a few moments everybody stood still, not knowing what to do next. Then some lads got up on lampposts to shout instructions. Those in charge took us along Kingsway towards Martha's nightclub. The police had lost all control and could do little more than watch.

As we walked up the Kingsway we neared at least 200

Swansea outside Martha's and lined up across the road. They stood their ground for as long as they could. Cardiff threw themselves into the enemy and the Swansea never really had a chance. I swear I saw tears in the eyes of some of them as they were kicked and punched all over the place. Other Cardiff chased more Swansea past the Queen's, one of their favourite pubs. This was utter annihilation. Some lads at the back of our mob never even saw what was going on, so big was the crowd in front of them. The Swansea started disappearing, leaving friends strewn on the floor, shop windows smashed and even some cars overturned. The police only began to regain a semblance of order when we made our way through the town and back to the train station. I hugged just about everybody I knew before returning to my minibus.

There have been Cardiff-Swansea confrontations since then – with mainly the police winning – but I have never seen anything to match that day. The Jacks hate Cardiff so much that many would deny they were destroyed in that free-for-all. However, I did speak to one of their main faces a few years ago and he admitted that we terrorised them. The national papers condemned the "scum" for a week after the match and the Mayor of Swansea told the *Daily Mirror* that it was the most violence he had seen since World War Two. Ask any football lad who has been involved in something like that and he will say it beats the best drug you can ever have. That's why people fight at football and that's why so many were out for it that day.

SWANSEA'S MAIN LAD through the 1990s was Mildred. In 1990-91 he was actually manager of a trendy clothes store in Swansea, a venture which didn't last long due to the poor number of dressers in the city. He had to do the occasional shift at its sister shop in Cardiff and, being young and keen at the time, we loved to wind him up. It was always hilarious him denying who he was. He will also recall the fake shotgun put to his face outside Martha's night club in Swansea one night after one of the boys got beaten up there. He wasn't to know it was a fake. The lad who did it was knocking off a girl in Port Talbot. One morning he got the train back to Cardiff and looked up the carriage to see 50 Swansea with Mildred sitting at the front. They made eye contact and he saw Mildred pondering, *Where do I know him from?* Needless to say, our lad didn't stay on the train for long. I spoke to Mildred a few times and he's the only Jack that has held his hands up and admitted they could never compete with us.

In fact they have a bad reputation for pointless attacks on innocents or small groups. One notable example came when they were travelling to Derby in the Worthington Cup. They stopped near Cardiff and popped into an Asda supermaket. Some of them started abusing a young Cardiff fan, causing a commotion big enough for the police to be called. Their bus was stopped from going any further, so they went into Cardiff city centre to further abuse office workers and normal law-abiding people. Another classic came before they played Millwall away, when their so-called top boy put flyers and posters around the city centre advertising their intentions, thus ensuring the police would shadow their every move and afford them plenty of protection.

I grew up with some Jacks myself in the Valleys and some are as good as gold but most of them are very naive when it comes to football hooliganism, with little going on upstairs. They have also been heavily into the British National Party, Ulster Unionism and far-right politics: racist fools stuck firmly in the 1970s with their pointless views. A few racist idiots have followed Cardiff over the years but they don't last very long. This is also one of the reasons why the Jocks rarely follow the Welsh national side abroad, unlike Cardiff.

CHAPTER FOURTEEN

City in Europe

EUROPE IS THE place to be and until recently Cardiff got into the Cup Winners' Cup quite often thanks to qualification via the Welsh Cup. Now UEFA, in their wisdom, have changed the rules so that you must be in the Welsh League to play in the Welsh Cup. Until that happened, we had some good adventures abroad. It was also the case that, by the late '80s, a lot of foreign clubs were developing their own hooligan gangs, who relished the chance to have a go at the Brits.

One Soul Crew episode actually came at a Swansea vs Panathinaikos Cup Winners' Cup game in the late '80s. The first leg in Greece made national news when 30 Swansea ended up in prison after taking a hefty beating. There was a media frenzy for the return leg, with Swansea out in force to look for some revenge. Thirty Soul Crew didn't want to be left out. They drank in Swansea before the game and even went behind the goal in the away end, where they soon made themselves known and a big fight broke out. They chased Swansea down the terrace with the Jacks clambering to get away. The police then cornered the Soul Crew and escorted them out and the boys drove back to Cardiff unscathed and happy.

The first European run I was involved with was in the 1988 season. Granted, our "runs" usually lasted just a couple of games but were a welcome distraction from mundane northern grounds. Our Welsh Cup final against Wrexham capped a superb season and was played at Swansea's Vetch Field on a glorious late-May evening. We had up to 5,000 there on two sides of the ground. Wrexham brought maybe 400 dismal supporters while Swansea too had a little turnout in the North Bank, which was allocated for them on the day. They were run ragged before the game but at least had a go at defending their city.

It was the third time that season that I had been to the Vetch with Cardiff and I was loving every minute of it. We won 2-0 with goals from our former captain Terry Boyle and Alan Curtis, who arguably is Swansea through-and-through but had a spell with us and that night scored one of the best Cardiff goals I have seen. He is now back at Swansea on the management team. Our reward in the Cup Winners' Cup was Derry City, of Northern Ireland. At that time Cardiff fans were banned from travelling away and only a handful managed to reach Derry and get tickets for the home end. We drew 0-0 and in the second leg were too strong for them, smashing them 4-0. Derry brought quite a big support but there was not a hint of bother and I recall a lot of scarf swapping and back smacking after the game.

We next drew Aarhus of Denmark. They weren't the biggest of clubs but played us off the park at Cardiff. Somehow we scraped a draw. I couldn't make it for the return leg – being only 17 I couldn't get the funds together – so I was gutted and I remember thinking I wouldn't let it happen again. The news and papers were full of tales of Cardiff fans rampaging on the ferry (Kenny, Gareth and the Aberdare boys on tour again). Whilst they were in Denmark I don't think they had any bother with the locals; it was over-exuberance with drink, no doubt. We lost 2-0 and our European ride was over once more.

Seasons later we were drawn against Admira Wacker of Austria. At the time the Grange End terrace was open for us and it was crammed full that night but with the front gate open for safety reasons. Wacker took the lead in the first half but in the second a free-kick was floated into their box and Chris Pike put in a bullet header to equalise. Good old Pike; he would have the most timid of Cardiff fans tearing their hair out. One game he'd miss sitters from two yards and the next he'd score with a 25-yarder. I was one of the first on the pitch followed by hundreds of celebrating city fans, and saw myself on *Football Focus* that Saturday falling in the penalty area. They held on for a 1-1 draw and the word was everyone would meet in Vienna for the second leg. I was definitely going but I couldn't make it for the week so I flew out on the morning of the game.

The night before was apparently eventful, with 30 Cardiff, including Karl and the Legend, battling with 30 Austrian skinheads outside a bar. The local Nazi divs got chased out onto the street and one turned and pulled out a gun. Nobody knew if it was a replica or not but Karl, a pure fruitcake, went for him anyway. The local hero crapped himself and ran with the rest of them into the darkness. City had over 700 at the Admira stadium with what seemed well over 100 lads. There were no local boys about anywhere. Cardiff eventually lost 2-1 after a spirited display.

In 1993 we were drawn against Standard Liege of Belgium and for the boys who knew the score this was a plum tie. For weeks after the draw, the talk was Liege, Liege. I knew we'd have a cracking rollcall and the Cardiff didn't disappoint. Loads had agreed to meet in Brussels on the Sunday night, have a night or two there, then head to Liege. Having been there twice with Wales I knew Brussels city centre pretty well and so did a lot of the boys. I fell in love with the place.

Different groups of Cardiff were arranging different things but me and two of my mates, Steve and Rob from Aberfan, arranged to go with a minibus full of potty fans from Cwm, Ebbw Vale, led by Nigel, as staunch a City fan as you will ever meet. These are all superb lads and the crack was guaranteed.

We drove to Cwm and the pub was open early Sunday morning. Also with us was Rory from Merthyr, an avid City nut and a fabulous feller. Tragically he's not with us anymore but that's one Cardiff fan who will live on in many people's hearts.

As soon as we left Ebbw Vale the crates were opening and the skunk was being rolled. I thought I'd also get the party going with a load of strawberry acid tabs. Nowadays I couldn't dream of it but not that long ago it was the norm. On the bus was Simon, a tattooist well into this thirties, and a bloke called Mike who was 42 and married. We all did acid straight away except the driver. Simon and Mike had only ever done it once previously, years ago. It didn't take us long before most of us were laughing our bollocks off but Simon and Mike still hadn't come up so in their wisdom they decided to buy some more off me. By the time they started tripping they had done two and a half each. They were completely out of their skulls. At one stage the laughter didn't stop for what seemed like an hour.

We had to go to a service station – I can't recall which ones but I'm sure they were in England somewhere – and one of the lads on the bus had to meet his sister, who had money for him. He couldn't even manage to get out of the bus to see her. The driver had to collect the money while the lad's sister stood in bewilderment wondering why he wouldn't come out and why everyone was laughing at her. The rest of that ride I don't remember much about, apart from a little stop in Staines and me having the munchies for miles until we finally found a petrol station. I think I bought about a tenner's-worth of food and drink and polished it off all at one go, like a trainee Homer Simpson. Seconds later I told the driver to pull over and ended up collapsing on the side of the road. Oh happy days, and this was just the start.

The 42-year-old Mike had lost it completely by now and convinced himself we were going to Blackpool, which was the weekend after. In Dover he lost his passport and, after initially panicking, he forgot all about it and ended up on the conveyor belt doing a Superman impression. In the departure lounge was an East German backpacker with a guitar who couldn't speak English but knew the words to some Bob Dylan songs. We sang with him for a while. We boarded the ferry, with Cardiff everywhere, and the party continued. There was a disco onboard but I had to go in the casino and ended up losing most of my money – surprise, surprise. After disembarking at Ostend we drove to Brussels and found a reasonable hotel close to the Grand Place, the attractive, bar-lined central square which is the usual vantage point for lads who visit Brussels.

On the Monday morning some of us wanted to check out the shops. The Belgian designer Dries Van Noten was "in", with some superb but very expensive knitwear. The Belgians were looking at me crazy when I enquired about it but eventually we found a store that stocked it and I borrowed £200 off one of my generous mates for one of his pieces, a thick red knit which became a cherished part of my wardrobe. We kept bumping into people across the city and most arranged to meet in one of the main bars in the square in the evening. After getting changed in the hotel we moved to the square, had some food and went for a butcher's in the red light area (as you do). As I was returning 30 minutes later I saw three police vans, with lights flashing, speeding towards the square. I didn't have to think twice to know what was going on.

As I got there, everyone in my minibus, bar one, was handcuffed against a wall and was then being led into the back of wagons. I found it quite amusing seeing Steve, Rory, Rob and the rest trying to argue their case with the *gendarmie*, who didn't give a fuck. The Belgian police obviously have no tolerance of British fans since fighting caused such a tragedy there at Heysel in 1985.

I found some other City and we went to the nick to see what the score was. The lads had been fighting with a load of Turks who had congregated in the square. They were going to be in all night and had to doss in the same cell with other City. Eighteen of them spent the night in one room. It wasn't the first time that Cardiff had had trouble with the Turks in Belgium. The boys told me later it was a proper nightmare in the cell but at least they were let out in the morning with slapped wrists.

After a night of drugs and prostitutes, match day arrived. The minibus was left in Brussels and we took the train in and got into Liege at about two in the afternoon. As we came out, fans in City shirts were everywhere and it didn't take us long to find the boys. There was a bar 500 yards into the main street, near the station, where all the usual Cardiff suspects were holed up. Loads drank merrily outside on the pavements For us, this was the pinnacle: Cardiff in Europe with your mob. This was the buzz. There were up to 300 boys in and out of the pub, 200 hardcore with another 100 who would join in at a push. The word was that the night before City had trashed some Liege in the pub opposite the station, but they were rated pretty game as foreign mobs went and would be up for it that afternoon.

A lad stood next to us in a long, silver Stone Island coat. I recognised him from a recent documentary about England fans called *Wake Up England*, in which he was shown with a group of Scottish casuals. I'm really good with faces and he was shocked that I recognised him. He had come all the way from Stranraer. He was there for an hour then abruptly disappeared. I think he may have been accused of being undercover. If he was, he was the smartest undercover cop I have ever seen. Talking of police, the full South Wales contingent were there along with Shakespeare, the NCIS (National Criminal Intelligence Service) officer assigned to City for a number of years.

One of our boys weeks earlier had been told by an English lad about a German called Ronald who followed Cologne but was obsessed with British teams, especially Chelsea and Hibs. We heard that he would be in Liege to have a drink and a chat with City but it completely slipped my mind until 5pm, when someone said that this German lad was going to get lynched in a pub by Legend of Cwmbran. We ran to rescue him from the wrath of one of Cardiff's maniacs, who was ready to knock him out. We intervened and all calmed down when we explained who he was and who he knew. He seemed all right but you never could tell. As it happened, this German arranged to join some Cardiff for a meet we had with the Jacks in Neath when we were banned from away games. In the end only 12 of us were left when we bumped into Swansea and we got chased right through Neath by a mob of 80 intent on killing us. Guess who joined them in the chase? Ronald the Kraut. I think he turned up and just mobbed up with the biggest firm he could see. He's been back since, got a slap and it was left at that.

Ronald is an interesting character, albeit a cheeky one. On a Saturday he would go to Marseille with the Paris St Germain firm, on the Wednesday he'd be in Legia Warsaw for a fight in Poland, then back home to Germany to have a nose there. He's got to be the most travelled football lad in the world: I heard a story last year that around the time of Nato's bombing campaign in Belgrade he went to see his mates at Red Star for a pre-arranged fight with the hooligans of Partizan. He has contacts with Antwerp, Feyenoord and many others, and is big mates with a Chelsea pal of mine called Pat. Some people think he is a copper. Who knows? Who gives a fuck, really? I know a few obsessed lads but he takes the biscuit.

Anyway, back to Liege, some locals came and passed in ones and twos as the afternoon wore on. They were dressed in typical foreign attire: big chevignon-type biker leather jackets – and these were the smart ones. A big blond lad approached

Platform-wearing loons stick the boot in at the infamous Cardiff City-Manchester United clash in 1974, a watershed in British football hooliganism. The Red Army invaded South Wales but got more than they bargained for.

Changing fashions: some young Cardiff casuals at Derby County in the 1985-6 season.

Tony Rivers enjoying himself one evening in Swansea after a derby clash in 1991. The Jacks were our bitterest rivals but on this night their city was taken over.

A sea of Cardiff on the pitch after winning promotion in 1993. City have been a yo-yo side for decades and have never achieved their potential.

Tony Rivers (far right) with a bunch of mates at Plymouth away in 1994. The day was to culminate in an extraordinary brawl with Plymouth's Central Element gang outside a pub.

Shakespeare, the NCIS intelligence officer who tailed us for years, taking some sneaky video footage.

CONGRATULATIONS
You've just been
Visited by the
CARDIFF CITY
SOUL CREW
UNDER 5'S

CONGRATULATIONS
You Have Just Been
Visited By The
CARDIFF CITY SOUL CREW

Obligatory calling cards for the Soul Crew and the younger Under-5s. Whoever started the trend for these – possibly West Ham –they caught on very quickly.

Trouble on the Bob Bank between Cardiff City fans and the police at a home derby against Swansea City in the 1996-7 season.

Just about to go off with Darlington at the last game of the 1996-7 season, when two coachloads of Cardiff "stumbled" across their pub. The Darlington are facing the camera.

A large Soul Crew flag at Oslo, Norway. European trips have been among the best moments following the Bluebirds and Wales.

Tony (centre) with mates at the Legia stadium in Warsaw, Poland, in 2000.

Millwall at home in 1999, and unprecedented numbers of Cardiff fans gather before the game. It goes without saying that none of the lads featured in this photo would ever dream of causing trouble!

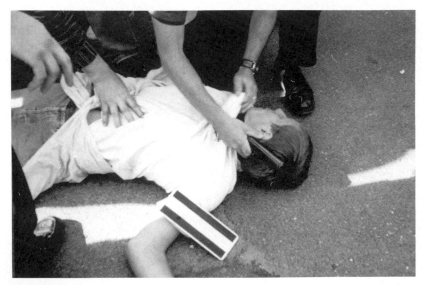

The Millwall game was the subject of huge pre-match hype and dire warnings of hooliganism. Those fears were realised when some Millwall burst out of the ground at the end of the game, only to receive a bad beating from hundreds of Cardiff.

The return fixture that season at the New Den saw the biggest police operation ever for a league match in Britain. Here mounted officers chase a mob through the south Bermondsey streets.

Celebrating promotion on the pitch at York in May, 2001. With Sam Hammam in charge, there is great optimism for the first time in decades. He was good enough to treat some of the Soul Crew to a champagne reception (inset) later.

The infamous pitch invasion after our FA Cup victory over Leeds United in January 2002. It led to a string of arrests but in truth there was little serious trouble.

us who had good English and said we'd have to wait as Liege were getting it together. He seemed nervous and in awe of the size of our mob. Liege have a big reputation in Belgium along with Antwerp, Bruges and Anderlecht and he told us they could pull up to 200. The police obviously knew him as they followed him everywhere.

Then it happened. Around 20-30 Liege came marching around the corner from the bar that had been destroyed the night before. There weren't many police there at that moment and the first 50 City ran into the middle of the road to confront them. They threw little bottles of cheap Belgian lager then, like any English firm, they stood and had it toe-to-toe until the rest of Cardiff in the pub realised what was going on and ran to join in. I was expecting many more Liege to come out of the pub to back them up as they were getting chased back around the corner. They got outside the pub where there were plant pots and road works laid out for them. They started throwing everything at us but one last charge sent them back inside the bar. I didn't notice the Belgian police arriving while Cardiff tried to smash the doors in

I sloped off as the police pushed Cardiff away and they started retreating back to their own bar. Many, many police vans started to arrive and their approach seemed to change from softly-softly to almost paramilitary in seconds. The vans parked outside the station and hordes of riot police ominously lined the streets, blocking the road where City were drinking. I sneaked off, knowing something was about to go down.

Hundreds of officers formed a cordon where Cardiff were drinking. No one was allowed to leave the club and soon people were being frogmarched into convict carriers. I stupidly went back to see what was going on. Some of my minibus lot were getting nicked again and I started waving and laughing. They had the last laugh when one of them called over to a copper and said, "He's with us." I walked quickly away smiling, only to be grabbed seconds later by two burly coppers. "Com vis us," they said. As I got near the boys started laughing. So much for "all for one and one for all".

They put us in plastic handcuffs, the ones that tighten the more you struggle, and we were crammed into the back of this van. I ended up arguing with Carwan, one of the lads from Aberfan, who I was cuffed to, as he was pulling and it was getting tighter. I'd have chinned him if I could. They eventually took us to army barracks and placed everyone in a massive gym with barbed wire all around and a big water cannon in the hall. It all seemed prepared and 150 Cardiff were detained. I had seen fights ten times as bad with fewer arrests but they weren't taking any rubbish today.

A Cardiff fan who was Belgian or French and could hardly speak English, but was covered in City badges, had a radio to listen to the game. He got a reception just before half-time and shouted in a French accent, "Liege one, Bluebirds two." The place erupted. All the lads I knew were there, rotten drunk, and it was that crazy we could have been on the away end. The police shook their heads while putting the water cannon on Def Con Three, ready to fire. As we came near the barbed wire, over 100 of us were doing the conga.

We were led off in small groups to have our photos taken. Everyone was "on one" by now and taking the piss out of the police. I think most of the photos had people pulling faces or sticking fingers up. My mate Steve was worried that he hadn't had his photo taken and even tried to ask an officer when it would be his turn. Moments later we got back to our friend with the radio. It was reality time: City were 5-2 down. Those few moments of joy are priceless, but are very few and far between – which makes them even sweeter.

Most of the lads' bags and stuff were back in Liege or Brussels but I had a sneaky feeling we would be deported – and I was right. Around 10pm we were taken to the train station and guarded all the way back to Ostend. Our minibus was also still in Brussels, so we found an all-night bar and waited for it. When we got back to Dover a BBC news crew tried to interview people about what happened but everyone was too tired to speak and just wanted to get back.

The telly and papers once again had a field day: "200 Cardiff fans run riot abroad," was just one of the headlines. At the time we were on everyone's lips after trouble at Port Vale and Fulham, among others. The Saturday after Liege, City were at Blackpool and few boys travelled, mainly because it was so soon after Liege. Some still managed to get themselves jailed. Some of my lot were nicked for the third time that week when they bumped into a mob of Leicester Baby Squad and chased them all along the Golden Mile. Police arrested 25 City. A nice, quiet week.

Apparently Liege brought a firm to Cardiff but their coaches were well policed and no-one saw them. The next month saw Arsenal take an off-the-pitch beating out there. They must have been better prepared for the Gunners than they were for us.

CHAPTER FIFTEEN

Court in the Act

THE 1993-94 SEASON was a busy one. We had just gained promotion from the Third Division, had been drawn against Standard Liege in Europe and had Fulham in our first away game. The West Londoners had a small, meaningless crew and so the target for the main lads was their near-neighbours Chelsea. Chelsea were at Ipswich but we knew that somewhere that day they would have a firm hoping to have a crack at us. I took the 8.25am train. It was full, as expected. Our first port of call was the Pride of Paddington pub and by noon we had a mob of 400 between the Pride and the Dickens. It was a sunny day, so the battle dress was Lacoste stripey polos and shorts. I had on a red Moschino sweatshirt, a label that had a few months' wear but went a bit gay overnight *a la* Versace.

A mob that big is impossible to keep together, especially us and especially in London. I ended up with around 25 but it was "quality": Neath Punk, Mark B from Ely, Stevie Weasel, Dave, Sherbet, Aitch, Beefy, Dibble and the Roath men. We caught the Tube at Slone Square and walked up onto the Kings Road, mingling in with the West London wealthy and the Saturday shoppers. We jumped in cabs and made our way to a Putney pub called the Cricketers. It looked like we had missed some bother, as a window was broken and we could hear sirens in the distance. We found out there had been a small skirmish between some of ours and a handful of Londoners.

Walking through the park to the ground we saw Cardiff everywhere: 3,000 had made the trip. Outside the ground was hectic. Some of us couldn't be bothered queuing and sat on a wall opposite. I got into a conversation with one of the boys, only getting up when I saw the last of the queues go in. I followed and paid to get in at a corner turnstile, assuming they had opened it up for us. I honestly didn't realise it led to a Fulham section. I soon realised my mistake but I wasn't the only one – there must have been 30 Cardiff at least on this packed Fulham terrace. There seemed to be an awful lot of local "lads" in there too. It was only going to be a matter of seconds before the inevitable.

City kicked off and immediately forced a corner. "Bluebirds, Bluebirds," came the chant not only from our main contingent behind the goal but also from the people standing next to me. A local ran through the crowd and punched one of the Cardiff fans in the head. Hello. It erupted into a massive fight. At first it was a flurry of punches and kicks, all a bit messy with everyone crammed together. Then a gap opened, schoolyard-style. I could only imagine this to be a throwback to the end-storming antics of the '70s. Cardiff began to get on top, led by reliable Ricky and Gerwin from Bangor, who were going nuts, but the Londoners traded blow for blow.

This was unbearable for the huge mob of Cardiff behind the goal. They started hurdling the fences and haring across the pitch. In 30 seconds flat, 200 had joined us, to screams of, "Come on you Cockney bastards." That was it. The Londoners' bottle went and the whole end turned and ran, many falling over each other as they did so. They were punched and kicked along the terrace to the halfway line. The police lost it completely, clearly overwhelmed by the numbers.

Both teams were taken off for half an hour. We made our way onto the pitch and over the fencing to the away end as some cops tried grabbing and nicking the boys. This lit the flame for more trouble; a gate was charged and the police and stewards were attacked. Neil Kinnock (yes, the very same) came around pleading for calm. It did cool down eventually and the players returned. Kevin Ratcliffe, our captain at the time, shouted, "Fuck off you wankers," in our direction but Nathan Blake clenched his fist and had a big grin on. We went on to win 3-1 with Blakey grabbing a brace. We must have geed him up.

After the game we returned to Paddington and that evening found out about Chelsea. A vanload of Cardiff stopped off for a drink on the Fulham Palace Road and were approached by 20 Chelsea. They must have thought it was Christmas but the Headhunters could not have bumped into a worse group anywhere: Viking, Jonny, Farrell, Mark T and the Prince from the Docks, with Darren, Kirse and other Barry boys, rounding off an awesome unit. When you get the Docks and Barry together it is like mixing Stella Artois and Strongbow: a lethal combination. By all accounts the first two Chelsea were knocked out cold and the rest backed off, realising they had picked on the wrong people.

The media had a field day, with Jimmy Hill calling Cardiff fans "a disgrace to football". Today's headlines are usually tomorrow's chip wrappers but for me the story would not end there. At dawn on a Tuesday morning in October, there was a loud thud at my front door. I looked out to see two police vans parked outside. I let them in. It was Fulham and Chelsea CID, with some of Cardiff's "spotters". They searched the house and cuffed me into the van. They wouldn't stop yapping, asking this and that. Two of them got talking about Chelsea, the lads they worked alongside, and said how Tottenham were the new governors of London. *Big deal*, I thought. It was too early to give a toss.

They took me to nearby Fairwater nick. The Met had based themselves there for a week and arrested 25 Cardiff fans in connection with the Fulham game. I was charged with affray. I saw the video of what I had been charged with: booting someone up the arse as they turned to run.

Into the nick walked Shaky, the NCIS officer. "Alright Tone?" he said. "Did you enjoy them reports?"

"Which reports," I enquired, playing dumb. He was referring to NCIS files of every fight of the previous season. A Wrexham lad at university near London had been doing a project on football violence and had apparently liberated them from the NCIS building. I ordered a copy pronto from my Wrexham contacts but never saw them. However, I wasn't about to admit anything.

"Which reports?" he said, smiling, to another officer. "These lads don't miss a trick, do they?"

It baffled me how he knew that I knew about them. Some of the more paranoid football lads often claim their phones are tapped and they may be right.

I was accompanied to court by Gareth from Aberdare who was on the same charge. Our solicitor told us they wanted scapegoats but that if we pleaded guilty they would take it down to threatening behaviour. *Great*, we thought, as long as I didn't get banned from the City. A small fine and a slap on the wrist I could live with. We had to go to court for a second time. "No problem," our solicitor said. "A fine and a possible ban, you're going to get." The judge clearly hadn't read the script. He gave us two months in jail.

I was gutted. We were taken down and driven to Wandsworth Prison, where we would serve 28 days. It was an utter nightmare. I feel sorry for the poor bastards who are there for years, because it felt like a year we were there for. It is a different world, You know what they say though, "If you can't to do the time, don't do the crime." It did teach me one valuable lesson: Plead guilty to fuck all!

On the first night in Wandsworth, Gareth and I were put in a cell with two of the most intimidating black guys you could ever meet. We hardly said a word, just glancing at each other occasionally and shaking our heads. They were soon trying to bully money off us for the canteen and for tobacco. I also overheard one pleasant conversation they had about cutting someone up in the showers.

Eventually we were moved to our own cell but then I think they just forgot about us. We were brought food in our cell at mealtimes and were let out an hour a day for exercise but otherwise we didn't see another soul. We didn't get a shower for nine days. At night we could hear the two men in the next cell shagging each other senseless. It was horrible.

Whilst wallowing in our misery we missed the Jacks at Ninian Park a few days before Christmas, not to mention the Spice of Life party the same evening. It was a game Swansea became quite proud of. They arrived late, sang a few songs on the way to the ground and began to rip seats out of the Grandstand and throw them like Frisbees, hitting young children in our family enclosure. Two hundred Cardiff then invaded the pitch and ran over to the Swansea, calling them down. They refused, as they were happy enough beating the seats up. Forty of their firm had turned up off the train at 7pm with no escort, only to be chased through town. Some of their better-known people were even spotted locking themselves in the cubicles of the men's toilets at Central Station. It must have been something they ate.

Some Swansea bright spark also made a video-cassette of camcorder clips of them rioting at Reading, Wycombe and one or two others. It was played in pubs around Swansea and fell into the hands of the police, who gleefully identified some of those filmed and arrested them. Very clever, lads. The Christmas derby also led to more raids for Cardiff. That season the authorities had had enough. National news had been made for incidents at Fulham, Liege, Blackpool (with the Leicester Baby Squad) and Port Vale. Eventually 350 exclusion orders were made from Ninian Park.

One funny story from the Cardiff-Swansea raids was about

Matty, a half-American, half-Cheltenham fruitcake. On being interviewed, he pleaded innocence. "Matty" the copper said, "We've got you on video goading Swansea down with your hands." His excuse was that he'd heard there was a fire, so he had got onto the pitch and gone to the Swansea end to call women and children down first. Priceless.

Myself and Gareth were finally released from prison on Christmas Eve. I had lost about two stone. It stopped me in my tracks for a while football-wise – though I never stopped following City – but soon I was falling back into my old ways. And my experience at Fulham certainly did not prevent me returning there on a Friday night a few years later. Two full coaches of lads arrived at mid-afternoon and drank from the Fulham Palace Road up to Putney. Eventually the Met turned up. The usual faces were there, including Shaky again and the Chelsea spotters. I had seen them a few times since prison at Cardiff a while and one or two Chelsea v Liverpool encounters.

As we left a pub we were put in a massive escort, with vans, motorbikes, dogs and possibly two officers to each of us. They walked us over Putney Bridge then stopped my group at the front. Two coppers came over with their senior officer, who wore a peaked cap. I thought they were taking the piss when one of the officers said, "Sir, this is Mr Rivers." The big cheese in charge said, "Hello Mr Rivers, I'm sorry for the inconvenience but we have to search everyone of you. I'm really sorry." We just shook our heads and laughed. At the same time, the River Thames was suddenly awash with speed, coke, joints and a few cans of CS gas as some of our merry men discreetly cleared their pockets. Better to lose a few quid than spend a night in the cells.

SPENDING TIME IN jail is not something I would ever want to do again, but I suppose it did help to cement my own reputation within the Soul Crew. So too did mixing it with some of the bigger-name firms in the hooligan world. As

Dave has already described, one mob who could give anyone a problem on their day was Portsmouth. The 6.57 Crew had been known for doing the business around the country for many years and had crossed our path a few times in the 1980s, though they seemed to have quietened down a bit by the mid-90s.

I came up against them occasionally at friendlies and cup ties. The first occasion was a friendly at home in 1990 (the Summer of Love). I had just shaved off my ludicrous bobbed hairstyle for a crew cut and Psycho and myself went in Block D of the Grandstand to check out Pompey's following. It was a surprise to see that they had loads of fans there for a nothing game. The bellringer was with them; he must go everywhere.

Just after kick-off, a group appeared up the steps. One after another they came past. A good 25, all in their mid-twenties, in what was then pretty exclusive Stone Island. We disappeared out of the stand over to the Bob Bank to inform people that they were there but there was hardly anyone about. At the end, we left and walked outside the away end. No police but no 6.57 Crew either. They had gone. We jumped in cars and drove towards town. We saw ten of them, one of whom immediately spotted the car, and parked up. As they turned the corner of the bridge into the station, we walked behind them. They saw six of us. One shouted to me, "Oi, big ears, fuck off," so we just walked quickly towards them. We got close and they were goading us on. We were all young but we were willing to have a go. A police van drove by the side of us, which alerted the Pompey. I think the police saved us really. I can't swim and I had visions of me getting thrown over the bridge, which I didn't really want.

As fate would have it we were drawn against them in the League Cup in the September. The first leg at Ninian was quiet as no 6.57 turned up but we took a decent-sized mob down there. A couple of us went by train and began drinking in a pub in Portsmouth-Southsea. There were some City in there, including a Rhondda Marine who was off duty and was showing off his Cardiff tattoos. We left for the station around 6pm to go up to Fratton. Five dressers walked ahead on to the platform. There were four of us and we ran towards them. First of all they ran and got to the top of the stairs, then turned. Matthew with me was swinging a walking stick. "Come on you English bastards," he was shouting. They were pretty game for it until one of them said, "We're Cardiff." I have seen a few situations like that, mistaken identity.

We then travelled to Fratton together and immediately bumped into our lot. We had about 50 and searched, looking for Pompey. We got to a pub called the Shepherd's Crook and three lads came out, including one with longer ginger hair who I recognised from the friendly. These three stood there as they were attacked in the doorway. They screamed for the people in the pub to come and help them, but to no avail. They did have a go back but they got hammered. One of the pub windows got smashed as Cardiff called for Pompey to come out but they wouldn't.

In the ground the 6.57 started to congregate but we had many more. Four of us who came by train from Aberdare bumped into a van full of our locals and we arranged to go back with them. After the game the main mob went one way and we went the other, with six of us lagging back from the rest. We got to the corner of a main road and several Pompey came around the bend. Gary M from Aberdare shouted, "Come on Pompey. We're Cardiff" As he said it, more and more of them came round. We were hoping it would be equal numbers but in fact had started on the front of their mob. They went straight for Gary, pulling his coat over his head and taking turns at punching him. We went to help him. There must have been 40 Pompey all over us but we stood. I hit one to the floor and he got back up and whacked me in the side of the head and I ended up on the deck. Matthew waded in with the walking stick and backed them off, amazingly. I couldn't believe that one or two of them actually had to scream at others to stand, as there was only six of us.

In the nick of time the police arrived and the Pompey dispersed. One officer told Matthew, "If I see you hitting anyone with that stick again tonight, I'll take it off you" The six of us all felt quite proud of ourselves and the story of our defiant stand did the rounds for quite a while. Pompey command a lot of respect in Cardiff and I doubt there is anywhere they haven't been and put on a show.

THE BIRMINGHAM ZULUS, of course, were another big-name firm. My next episode with them came in 1996, when they were relegated to Division Two. That summer my telephone number had been given out to one of them by a lad from Wrexham, and for weeks before the game I received non-stop threats that the Zulus were coming to sort Cardiff out.

The end result of all this verbal was, of course, that a monstrous firm of Cardiff turned out on the Boxing Day for them, with pubs in town and all the way to the ground housing large, nasty groups. Before the game, 500 Cardiff patrolled near Ninian Park ... but no Zulus. It was a massive letdown. We had all sorts of shady characters out and some of the Docks lads had a go at me because I had told them what the Birmingham had been threatening. I mean, how was it my fault they didn't turn up? Some people were just gutted they couldn't get hold of any.

Actually most of the Docks hate football but turn out in numbers for the decent crews when there is a chance of a big fight. What I have witnessed over the years is some of the Docks lads' punching power. These people could easily have had decent careers in the boxing rings. One Docks lad called Farrell reminded me of Thomas "Hit Man" Hearns. The first time I witnessed his punches was in Channel View Leisure

Centre in Grangetown, at the first legal indoor rave in Cardiff, in 1989. Myself, Hopkins and Julian traveled down to have a look. It was pure hard-core with a bouncy castle situated by the side of the dancefloor. The three of us took our shoes off and started bouncing away. On departure I took one bounce too many and fell off at possibly 50 mph and, as luck would have it, flew straight into Farrell, who was carrying two cups of boiling coffee. They went all over his shirt. He wasn't a happy chap and before I could apologize he grabbed me around the throat and pushed me onto the front of the castle. I bounced back up for him to give me a left jab, bounced back again for a right cross, then a final bounce back for a kick in the balls. I looked like a human yo-yo. I could have bounced in a different direction and got away but I think out of respect or fear I let him carry on the job.

There are at least ten Docks lads who turn up at the City who are serious fighters. Once at Peterborough we bumped into their firm in the town centre. Farrell knocked three men out cold in the space of a few seconds, while I was smashed across the head with a cycle chain and left barely conscious. I also remember 70-80 Peterborough getting battered and run by about 25 of us from a pub called the Lion, with the Docks lads doing most of the damage. Two Peterborough were out cold outside the bakery, getting dragged in by customers. Two pairs of legs slid through the door like something out of a Western.

Our trip to St Andrews was in April. We don't often get the chance to play teams like this away and when we do, we always show. Some of us made our way by car and got to New Street around 10.30am. There were already groups of black lads hanging around. I noticed one in a Stone Island coat, reading a paper. He looked like he was going to work or something, until he rolled up the paper and came over to us.

"Come on Cardiff," he said. "Outside."

There was only a few of us. We told him we were waiting

for our others. His mate came over. "Fuck off out of it you Brummie twat," came from behind me. It was early but they were out already. I walked up to the black lad and said, "Don't spoil it mate, our mob is due in just after eleven. Tell your boys to wait." All I got from him was a mouthful of abuse. Then he left.

Minutes later, five Cardiff came running into the station, one of them covered in blood. They said, "Help us, Help us. The fucking Zulus are coming" We ran out the front, only ten of us. There were around 50 Zulus getting chased off by the law. The lad who was bleeding was concussed and collapsed in the station. The bastards had really turned him over. I assumed Birmingham would have been more clever than this. After their antics with just a few of us, the police were straight on the scene. If only they had waited they could have had a crack at all of us.

By the time over 100 Soul Crew arrived just after 11am, the place was swarming with police. More Cardiff arrived in cars. This was an unbeatable mob, up to 150 in Birmingham city centre just after 11am, and no passengers. As word spread about the badly beaten lads, the Soul Crew were fuming. We marched out like a battalion, followed by the police, and got to Bar St Martins around the corner. One of the top Zulus, Al, was in the doorway on his mobile. "Get round here" he was shouting. "They got a right fuckin' crew." He was obviously telling the others. The police pushed us away as some tried to speak to him.

The escort to the ground took ages and we could see Birmingham appear now and again. We arrived at the ground before 1pm. The stadium certainly looked better this time around, with an all-seater away end. Just before kick-off, their mob arrived in the stand above us; another massive crew sat to our left. With 1,500 City fans packed in, the atmosphere was soon a bit lively.

Cardiff took the lead with a stunning strike from Paul

Millar that later won Endsleigh League Goal of the season. We went crazy. Bodies flew over the seats. As usual, however, the second half saw them strike back. They equalised and some of their boys came on the pitch. We climbed the fence but were hit back by police. They scored again. Lads tore seats out and threw them onto the pitch and up at the Birmingham above. It was boiling over as the Birmingham upstairs tried to wind us up and the police had to step in as both mobs held a seat-throwing contest.

The game ended and we were led out straight away into the car park, which overlooks the road where the home fans leave the ground. There was a big fence in the way. Missiles came over and were thrown back. The first 30 of us charged down and reached a gate at the side of the fence. For about a minute the 30 of us had it toe-to-toe with Brummies who were trying to get through. Two of them ended up on the floor as we bucked them away. More Cardiff arrived as the police tried to block the gate. Birmingham's mob kept passing and passing on this road, 1,000 at least, and very impressive, but we had similar numbers and weren't budging at all. We were kept in the car park for 30 minutes, until the bulk of the road was cleared, and then let out with a massive escort.

One or two Zulus came over for a chat and told us we were the first decent mob to go there in years. They also said they would do their utmost to get at us on the way back to New Street. The police cleared the streets well, however, and we didn't really see anyone, though after the game a coach full of Cardiff pissheads was ambushed and their bus wrecked. And after we left New Street, Bristol City – who were at Stoke – got off there and bumped into these Zulus. It was safe to say that was a big mistake.

The Soul Crew have always had respect for the Zulus and I believe they also hold us in high regard, especially after the "welcome" they recently received in Cardiff for their biggest game ever, against Liverpool in the Worthington Cup final of

2001. I also saw Birmingham in a much-publicised game with Millwall a few season ago, when they really had daft numbers out, and at an FA Cup tie at Leeds, where 250 of them turned up at 11am seemingly sponsored by Stone Island. After the game they were ambushed by about 400 Leeds, which was very entertaining to watch, Leeds possibly coming out on top.

CHAPTER SIXTEEN

The Road to Wembley

THE FA CUP is a unique competition, cherished as much by Welsh clubs as by English. By pitting together teams from all of the different divisions, and from outside the league, it creates an unparalleled sense of spectacle and drama, and throws up opportunities to visit towns and grounds you would never normally reach. For these reasons it has a special place in the affections of all football followers – including the hooligan element.

The first FA Cup away tie I saw with Cardiff was at Enfield on a Sunday in 1988. It was a heavily policed game at their tiny ground in North London. Over 1,500 City were there with a large contingent of lads in the then-popular uniform of Ralph Lauren knitwear, Armani jeans and Timberland. It was a cracking little atmosphere and apart from a few skirmishes the police looked after the invasion of the Taffs well. Cardiff went on to win 4-1 and that doesn't happen very often.

The season after we were drawn against Gloucester City at home. They brought a little mob but Cardiff didn't have much of a turnout so not a lot happened. Cardiff got lucky on the pitch, being 2-0 down with five minutes to go when up popped young Morris Scott to score two late, late goals. The Bob Bank went absolutely psycho and Gloucester away looked very appealing. I ended up going on a "normal" fans' bus from Merthyr and when we arrived it was clear that the police hadn't anticipated such an away following. The away end could hold just over 1,500 but another 2,000 Cardiff had turned up without tickets. As we queued to get in it was going off all around. Cardiff were staging running battles with the police and the locals were terrified – the Gloucester lads who had swaggered outside Ninian Park on the Saturday were in a completely different mood tonight. Hundreds of Cardiff tried to break down the home end gates to get in for free but were forced back by police and stewards. At one stage a mob of Gloucester was run across the terrace by 20 City fans. Cardiff won 1-0 and the papers condemned the rioting City fans.

Next season was a pretty plum draw for us, Queens Park Rangers at home. On the morning of the game, town was busy as hell. Cardiff lads were sniffing over by the station, scouting any Londoners who got off the trains. The only downtown pub near the station was rammed full with Cardiff. Only a few QPR lads showed and a couple of them took a few slaps. At the game the place was rocking, with a crowd close to 14,000 and the most people I had seen in the Bob Bank. David Seaman kept QPR in the cup with some superb saves. After the game I saw a vanload of QPR lads getting dragged out by about ten Cardiff. A couple of Docks lads were there and one had an axe but thankfully didn't use it. The van was smashed to bits.

I went to the replay in a Transit full of stereotypical Rhondda fruitcakes. We stopped in Cheveley services along with six coaches of the official CCFC Supporters' Club. It made national news as the services were ransacked and the staff fled in fear. I confess it was pretty disgusting behaviour – but rather funny nevertheless – as loads of fans emptied the shelves and even the till.

We managed to get to Loftus Road right on cue. The Cardiff already there had destroyed two pubs and hammered a load of QPR, and the police were stretched to the limit. Four thousand Cardiff were packed into the two tiers behind the goal. I was overwhelmed by such a following. The night before Swansea had played at Anfield and it certainly looked on television as though they had taken less support. City played really well but lost by two late goals. After the game around 400 Cardiff invaded the pitch, some getting to the halfway line before police intervened. David Seaman had to sprint as fast as he could to get away from the marauding Welshmen and the papers once again had a field day about another Cardiff City night of rioting.

The next season's Cup run saw us drawn against little Hayes, the non-league club from Middlesex. I had heard about Hayes previously and about how Swansea had a torrid time there when lads from other clubs turned up. When they came to Ninian we were scraping the barrel in the league and our support was dwindling. We were lucky to get a 0-0 draw and after the game four of us went for a drink in the Owain. As we sat outside, four lads came over and started mouthing. We couldn't believe it. We got up and walked over to them but before we knew it we were surrounded by 15 men, all in their thirties. "You better fuck off Taff, you're a bit out-numbered," one of them said. We took his advice and turned to run as they unleashed a barrage of punches and kicks. They gave chase for a bit but then gave up. I was embarrassed because my girlfriend at the time saw the whole thing. I thought she was going to see how brave and handy I was, not watch me being thrown about like a rag doll. I felt like a right pussy.

We ran round town to all the pubs looking for reinforcements but there was no-one about. We spotted the same Hayes lads walking back the train station and tried frantically to get a little mob together but with no luck. At that time only the diehards were following City: as it proved at the replay, which was to be played at Brentford's Griffin Park.

I travelled up with my friend Geraint and Mallo, one of the main Cardiff lot. As we pulled off the M4, the signs didn't look good. A Transit full of lads flagged us over and asked where the ground was. They weren't Cardiff fans but a bunch of moody-looking Londoners who had obviously travelled for just one thing. As we continued over the bridge and up towards the ground, there were lads everywhere but we didn't recognise any of them. It was one of them nights.

We went on the open terrace behind the goal, maybe 150 Cardiff fans with about 15 fighters. I think half of London's thugs turned out that night. They were everywhere: a real hate-the-Welsh night. We spotted QPR, Chelsea, Cockney Reds and some Arsenal, and they were just a few of the faces that turned out to greet us. I think they had expected an invasion after the support we had taken to QPR the year before.

Half an hour into the game, a mob of over 200 entered to our left. They had everyone with them: men, women, blacks, Asians. I think it was the Ladbroke Grove Lynch Mob. We began to feel very, very uncomfortable. Even so, we still had a good go at winding them up. To round it off, Hayes scored in the last minute and beat us 1-0. Ten of our main lads did get in their end though and had a little argument before the police escorted them out. After the game we had to endure walking back to the car through hordes of hair-trigger Londoners. We kept our heads down and got to the motor safely but of all the games and grounds I have been to, that night ranks as one of the dodgiest. Only when we were safely on our way home could we relax and admit we had been lucky to get out in one piece.

FOR A TRUE football fan, a run in the FA Cup is worth the season alone and in 1994 we had a mini-success, reaching the fifth round. It started when we beat Hereford 3-0 in the first round and then overcame Enfield again after a replay. We had been better prepared for the game over there than at Hayes: I sorted out a good coach out with some Roath on it, some good lads from the Valleys, Steve Weasel, Steve of Millbank and Little Colin. Although we met a couple of Tottenham after the game, they saw what we had and didn't really want to mix it.

The third-round draw brought a tie with Middlesbrough. They were then in the First Division so it wasn't quite the financial bonanza it would be now but many lads couldn't wait. Middlesbrough had a reputation as one of the best firms in England and I knew they would make Cardiff a big game. Others knew the same: word went around that these Boro don't mess about and would be trying to drink in our pubs. We would need a serious turnout to match them.

On the day of the game, a carfull of us drove through Westgate Street just after 11am. I was with the Aberfan lads. We saw Mark H and flagged him over. He came jogging up. "They're fucking here already," he said They were in the Albert pub, near the station. We drove off to park and when passing the pub we saw there were bodies everywhere, upstairs and down. They must have left the north-east pretty fucking early. We found out they had left at 4am. This is what I meant when I said we knew they had a serious firm. We parked up and walked past the pub. They had two lads stood in the doorway of the pub who saw us and smiled as we walked past. I looked back and one was still grinning at me and nodding.

We went into downtown after a while and Cardiff started milling around. Jonny of the Docks went into the pub to speak to the Boro and returned to tell us they had well over 100 and were "proper". They were a real firm who did things right: they made sure that we knew where they were but kept quiet about it, not making a fuss, just waiting for us to get a firm big enough to have a crack. This is why they have got tons of respect in the hooligan netherworld. If that had been Swansea, as soon as they got off the train they would have sung, "Jack Army," started on any Cardiff fan and basically caused a big commotion before they got near our lads.

I was pissed off with the turnout in town. This wasn't like us at all. By one o'clock we had only between 40 and 50. A large number of Cardiff boys were drinking near the ground, which was no good – we needed everyone in town. But we had to make a move soon. Simply, we had to attack the pub. We had made our way to the Owain to speak to some more lads and then decided to walk down Westgate Street. We still only had about 40, as some boys showed their true colours and stayed with their pints. We walked on down to the Albert and stood in the road outside. Some of our main lads were there, Viking, Rusky and some of the Docks.

We went for the doors and attacked the Boro in the doorway. They were getting done but all of a sudden we stopped and walked back to let them come out of the pub and fight properly. This was a mistake. The Boro who had been upstairs had by now charged down and came bowling out with everything they could lay their hands on. Bottles, stools and glasses came hurtling through the air. Loads of lads come out on to the road and it went off crazy as we stood. They kept coming and coming and so did the missiles. Then, all to a man, they charged. I will never forget that roar going up; they were the real deal. My eyes began to burn – I had taken some CS gas right in the face. I frantically blinked my eyes and shook my head and by the time I looked up we were backing off. They were all over us now and we had to retreat. Some Cardiff like Rusky and Joe from Barry refused to budge but they were getting kicked all over the place. We tried to make a stand but once we got turned that was the end of it and we had to retreat.

The police arrived and tried to round up the Boro firm. Traffic was at a standstill as this went on all around. They were the best firm I had seen come to Cardiff and our main older lads said not since Chelsea or Portsmouth had they seen a team so organised and game. Up near the ground we had hundreds but I was gutted and didn't want to speak to anybody. I was sick. I thought, *What's the point in all these people turning up near the ground when the action is already over?* I knew that the firm we had at the ground would have dealt even with the Boro mob but it was too late – the result was already theirs. Around 30 of the Boro did break out of their escort and walk past the Ninian. The pub emptied and the Boro were run to the corner of Sloper Road, with many receiving beatings. That did make me feel slightly better.

The game itself was a cracker, played in driving rain. Cardiff, thanks to Phil Stant and Gary Thompson, came back twice to snatch a 2-2 draw. We took a minibus up to the replay from Mountain Ash and there were also a couple of good private coaches booked. The boys were after some payback but as we approached Middlesbrough the local police pulled all buses onto a lay-by to escort us in. HTV News in Wales had reported that it was all-ticket, which turned out to be untrue but deterred a lot of people from travelling. The police used to do this quite often to keep the numbers down.

Ayresome Park was a pretty poor ground and over 800 City fans were packed in the corner of the away end. To our left and right were Boro lads. It was an intimidating place but we got into the swing of things, with the usual anti-English songs to wind them up. We were of course the underdogs but, true to the romance of the Cup and all that, we took the lead with a brilliant header from '90s hero Phil Stant after a great cross by Phil Bater. We held on for the lead as long as we could. Loads of nailbiting followed until, deep into injury time, Boro sneaked up and got an equaliser. The ground went bananas: one Boro fan was hanging from a stand up above and had to be rescued by stewards. No-one could see Cardiff winning in extra time but they proved us wrong. The Boro keeper somehow let a weak effort by Nathan Blake go through his legs. Cue another bonkers celebration. At the end the players came over and complete strangers were hugging me.

This is one thing about football – it brings so many people together.

After the game, our minibus had to go to the police station to pick up one of the boys who had been nicked for being drunk and disorderly. At the nick we were told we had to wait until one o'clock in the morning. Loads of Boro had also been arrested and as they were led out we had a good chat. They said the mob they took to Cardiff was their best since Chelsea away in the play-offs in 1987. They also took the same 100 to Pisa in Italy for an Anglo-Italian cup-tie. They were really sound lads and they went on their way. One amusing tale they told me was that when they had played at Tottenham, an ex-star at Middlesbrough who was injured went down with the firm and got into a spot of bother.

After waiting for our drunken pal we went to get a takeaway in the edge of town. As we left with our food, four lads came out of nowhere. One of them said, "Come on Taffy, where have you been?" Another one told us to walk down a road where some Boro were waiting. We said we were just going home and took a rain cheque on that one. It was 1.30 in the morning and they were still looking for it. Respect!

We were now in the fourth round and drawn at home to Manchester City. After season ticket holders had first bite, the remainder of tickets went on sale at Ninian Park on the Sunday before the game. Crazily, the club allowed four tickets per person, which meant that many loyal fans were left without. The queue went on for a mile but we got there early enough to ensure we got tickets.

On match day, everyone made sure they were in town early, packing all the pubs. It was a superb time to be a Cardiff fan; you have to savour such moments. Everyone turned out and there were Cardiff everywhere. There were some small skirmishes but no decent mob of Man City. The boys that did show got run. Looking at the away end inside the ground it did seem that they had a lot of boys but give

Cardiff a big game like this and no-one could touch the Soul Crew. It was a superb atmosphere, and in the second half Nathan Blake curled a dream goal in front of the Canton Stand to pull off an amazing giant-killing act. Our keeper Mark Grew even saved a penalty in the last couple of minutes to cap a remarkable afternoon. After the game you couldn't move in Sloper Road for lads, 1,000 at least. Most of Man City's lads were approached but they all declined the offer of fisticuffs. They dispersed very quickly and couldn't wait to get home, no doubt.

The fifth round, and it looked like we were going to play Newcastle, which everyone had their fingers crossed for, but they lost to Luton. Our fixture against the Bedfordshire team was at home and was moved to a Sunday. It saw another full house, apart from the poor turnout of Luton fans. They possibly had 30 lads but nothing impressive, Before the game we drank in Canton. There were a few hundred in the King's. I went out to get something to eat with little Mark from Ely and two taxis pulled up with eight Luton lads in. I asked where they were going and they had been told by some comedian outside Central station to head to the King's for a quiet drink. I said, "I'm not being funny lads but somebody's winding you up." I gave them directions to a genuinely quiet pub, otherwise they would have been slaughtered. Luton went on to knock out Cardiff and that fat Jack Hartson was lucky to get out alive after trying to wind us up. They went on to play Chelsea at Wembley. Chelsea vs Cardiff at Wembley, now that's a thought.

A couple of seasons after, we had fairly close Cup games at Swindon Town and Reading. Sometimes the police and Football Intelligence must be on different wavelengths, as it proved at Swindon. Around 100 Cardiff, a young, dressed firm, arrived in Swindon at 10.45am. One of the main people was taken to one side and asked if everyone would follow the police to a secluded pub out of the way. This lad explained that he wasn't going to try to tell the boys anything, and carried on. Two minutes later, he was arrested. The police enquired whether this was the bulk of our mob. They really were that ill-informed. Another 150 arrived an hour later, then more, and it was obvious the police didn't have the manpower to deal with it.

Cardiff left town and marched to the ground: a firm of 600 at least and with the shocked police force just observing. Some Cardiff were already there by minibus and coaches and had chased a load of Swindon near the ground. When you're in a mob this big you do believe you're invincible. I have travelled the length and breadth of Europe and witnessed nearly every firm and no-one has ever come near us for size. I know lads from Millwall, Chelsea, Leeds and Birmingham will argue the fact but that's their prerogative. Bias aside, I say it how I see it.

We ended up getting knocked out of the Cup 2-0. After the game we were kept in for five minutes, then all let out. It started to go off with the police as soon as we ran out into the car park. Hundreds of City charged up to the Country pub on the corner, which was surrounded by officers. They came under a hail of bricks and bottles. Swindon's mob were in the pub and as we walked past some of them tried to get out but were pushed back in by the plod. There was a tight cordon around the building and no way through. Then as we turned the corner there was a big roar and a mob came steaming towards us. We ran straight into each other and it took three boys getting whacked until we realised we were all Cardiff. After some apologies and a few jokes we all walked back to the station.

Everything was getting wrecked on the way back, as usual. This is a bit loutish, I know, and those involved are rarely the lads but part-timers who come out for the big games. Most of them the real boys wouldn't even recognise. Later on in the year, Radio 5 Live did a programme about football violence and had a reporter who was at the Swindon Cup tie. He was hiding behind the wall after the game with his microphone and all you could hear were roars and, "Come on you English bastards."

Reading didn't show when they played at Ninian, which was no great surprise. Cardiff got on the Grange End and stood with the Reading. They declared who they were but nothing happened until the police dragged them out. The replay was at Elm Park. Even though I had never seen them on numerous visits to the City, I knew Reading had a little mob and was pretty sure they would be somewhere that night. Cardiff started turning up early and when I arrived at five a couple of the lads were waiting and took us to a pub containing 200 Cardiff. A pub near the station had also been damaged, with the toilets wrecked. What was the point in that? That sort of silly vandalism got on my nerves.

We moved from pub to pub but the Thames Valley Police, who don't take any shit, shadowed us. The bulk of the mob left once more while 50 to 60 of the main Soul Crew stayed behind. The ploy worked, as the police left to keep tabs on the bigger mob. We got all the way to the ground without an escort, only to end up back in the clutches of the Old Bill. This kind of cat-and-mouse was a regular feature of our big games.

Outside the ground, a vanload of Llanishen told us they had come across 70-odd Reading and received a decent slap. They were led by an infamous Chelsea lad who was to be the unwitting star of the recent *MacIntyre Investigates* documentary. What bugged me was that the Soul Crew had been drinking in Reading for hours and hadn't heard a peep from Reading, then something like that happens out of the way.

There were 2,500 City crammed into the away end, while the bank to our left was packed with young Reading. Before the game started some Cardiff got bored and invaded the pitch. It went off in a corner with police and stewards but

Reading seemed reluctant to join in. The majority of Cardiff couldn't be arsed either. The game was a stalemate and went to the lottery of a penalty shootout. Within minutes, we were out of the Cup for a another year.

Afterwards, the bulk of City were escorted back to the station. Forty main men managed to sneak round to the home end and have a little wander. We saw nothing. As we walked back into town we saw three lads in Stone Island all in the same line of phone boxes, obviously hiding. One of the boys tapped the windows. They couldn't even speak with fright but we weren't going to turn the three of them over. Later one of the City who had been arrested told everyone that the Reading firm were being held near the nick by the local Bill. He said they were all made to sit on the floor for an hour.

"WEM-BER-LEY, WEM-BER-LEY, WE'RE the famous Cardiff City and we're going to Wembley."

The great thing about the new play-off system for promotion and relegation was that, for a perennial yo-yo side like Cardiff, it added spice to the end of the season. And in 1997, having forged our way into the play-off semi-final, we had our best chance of reaching Wembley since the 1988 Football League centenary tournament, when all we'd had to do was go to Orient and get a result there. We lost 4-1 and Tranmere qualified instead.

The play-off semis were two legs. Our fellow semi-finalists were Northampton Town, Wycombe and Swansea City, and we had Northampton. The local Press were relishing an all-Welsh Wembley final and so were we. Being a Cardiff fan is to see one false dawn after another but we always seem to fall for them. The first leg was at our place on a Sunday, an all-ticket early morning kick-off. Northampton had never showed before but I half expected their so-called Affray Team to turn up this time around, with it being the play-offs and everything.

I had been to Northampton at least twice and they usually had a turnout for us at home.

In the morning it poured down and I sat in the Grandstand with a few of the lads to watch City dominate in front of 12,000 fans. In the second half, disaster struck: one of their players broke from midfield and chipped the winner at the Grange End in front of a paltry 700 travelling fans. The final whistle went. Hundreds of Cardiff searched for any sign of a rival firm in the car park afterwards, to no avail.

The return game was on a Wednesday at the new Six Fields stadium at Northampton. It was a small, compact stadium and our allocation was laughable, only 800 tickets. This ruled out many lads. Most of our tickets went to season-ticket holders but some of the boys did manage to get tickets and I travelled up in the car with Andy and Steve Moog from Aberdare and Dave. A private coach took the faces up but I couldn't get off work till half past three, so I was picked up then and we made our way up as fast as we could. We arrived just before kick-off.

We bumped into the coach and Steve from Aberfan came over. They had just run Northampton. We got in and the ground was packed. Above the roof of the home end you could see hundreds of locals all congregating on a grass banking watching the game for free. We had a nightmare start to the game, going 1-0 down straight away and soon after being reduced to ten men. Amazingly we equalised and were all-square at half-time. But after the restart the Cobblers went ahead 3-1. I had suffered many miseries with Cardiff and no doubt will suffer many more but I have never been as gutted as this. I'd have rather not reached the play-offs than suffer this. With 15 minutes to go, some of us had had enough. There were loads of game lads there but only around 40 of us left. A lot of the boys just didn't want to know because of the disappointment.

We left the ground and marched around to the home end,

through the car park and past a few police on horseback who had their backs turned to us. There were hundreds of hundreds of people on the bank above the car park. We said nothing to each other; we all knew what we were going to do. We raced up towards the crowd on the banking and they all fled. A couple of our boys, Little A and Casey, had traffic cones and caught a couple of people on the back with them. The Cardiff in the ground could see hundreds of Northampton fans scattering with us running through them.

A gap appeared and loads of Northampton started coming back. This was their firm. *Brilliant*, I thought. We were too cocky. The cones we had thrown came flying back, with interest. They kept coming in wave after wave as we desperately fended them off. Soon there were bodies everywhere.

Neath Punk was floored and so was Wasp. Some Cardiff started to back off. "Where are you going?" I screamed, and they all ran back in. Two of them got decked. We were picking each other off the floor and piling back in, and managed to back them off again up the hill. One local had a bottle smashed over his head but he came straight back into us with blood drenching his Burberry shirt.

The police then came in to try to break it up. This was a full-on battle with hardly anyone taking a back step. It then started to go off with the police and us. This fight lasted nearly 15 minutes and they backed us off maybe ten yards in the whole time. They had the upper hand, I admit, because of their sheer numbers but they never did us. It didn't seem like it was your normal football lads either; they had some big local beefcakes. I remember one of them had a Gold's Gym vest on and was very handy.

The force batoned us into the car park but some of us ran around to the dual carriageway where the Northampton were heading. We ran up behind the Burger King. With the police between us, they started to throw missile after missile. It was dark by now and we were desperately trying to dodge the police and the bricks, bottles and stones. There was no more serious fighting, however, and we went away deeply disappointed about Wembley but with the consolation of a heroic ruck and with our heads held high.

CHAPTER SEVENTEEN

The Plymouth Brethren

I HAVE TO be somewhere else when Wales are playing rugby. Cardiff and the Valleys become a chamber of horrors, full of drunken, embarrassing freaks pissing and throwing up in the streets and wandering in front of traffic. I respect rugby even though I don't like it but some of the sport's Welsh supporters are morons, and worse than any football hooligan I've come across.

So when, in February 1994, our game at Plymouth Argyle fell on the same day as the Wales vs England rugby game, I couldn't wait to get away. I had been hearing for a while about Plymouth's gang, the Central Element, and had had a bit of an argument with some of them in the lower Grandstand when we had played them at home. We took a coach and had 33 on board, a good mixture of lads from all areas of South Wales: Aberfan, Neath, Port Talbot and Cardiff. Every person there could be relied on if things got out of hand. You could go away with 200 to 300 people and not know where you stood with half of them but I had grown up following City with these people. The driver, however, had no idea that there was a game on and was under the impression that we were going shopping for the day. He was more interested in talking about the rugby.

Plenty of lager and pills lubricated the journey. We arrived just after 11am to find no police waiting, a welcome change. The plan was to reach the town centre and stay low-key. We alighted on the edge of the main shopping street and easily blended with the crowds on what was a busy shopping day. First we headed into Cody Brothers, the menswear shop that sells essential clobber. The three staff working there stared transfixed, counting Stone Island after Stone Island coat entering their shop. They seemed a bit nervous because of the numbers but we weren't there to steal anything (as many football mobs have done in the past, not least when Wrexham and their Celtic friends looted the Lacoste shop in London). These assistants were decent guys and we asked them about the Central Element. They told us they didn't drink in town anymore.

We found a good pub in Union Street called Punch and Judy's and decided to stay there. After a short while I had itchy feet, so Rob and I decided to go for another look in the clothes shop. On approaching we saw four lads on the corner, all dressed in Stone Island. I walked across to them and before I could say anything they were already on the back foot.

"If you want us Plymouth, we're in Punch and Judy's," I said.

"Oh, we don't drink in town anymore,' replied one. "We'll be in the Britannia which is right near the ground."

They wanted us to walk all the way up there to them when we were in town without any police. The usual etiquette in these situations is that the onus lies on the home contingent to make the move: if you're in their town drinking with no escort then the ball is in their court. We had another nose in the shop and then went back to the pub, where we were told that the Plymouth we had just spoken to had turned up in a new Golf Gti and called out a couple of people for a chat. Some of the boys took this the wrong way and chased the English lads back into the car, then smashed the windows, which made them drive off a bit rapid.

The pub filled up with rugby fans and I was surprised to see how many were Welsh: they were oblivious to the fact that a Welsh football team was playing in Plymouth and were horrified that we were Welsh and not interested in rugby. We left and made our way through the town. Still no sign of the OB. There are certain times when you go away with your boys and you know nothing will stand in your way. This was one of those days. A few of the lads had taken some sniff and were ready for anything. We walked and talked past the train station. One or two of the boys took photos.

Up the big hill towards the ground, we were given directions to the Britannia pub by a local: "Carry on up the hill for around quarter of a mile and the pub stands right up on the top." As we approached the top the pub became visible. A few boys stood outside and a car full of lads drove past. What we couldn't see was that the pub was rammed full of their firm. Two or three Cardiff were in there having a quiet drink and later they filled us in later on what Plymouth were saying. "I can't believe it," one of them said, "They've got heads!"

We got closer. Plymouth clocked us and started bolting out of the pub towards us. Blondie from Roath, one of our main lads, said, "Just walk into them slowly and then give it to them big style." *Fuck that*, I thought. I put a sprint on. The first over was a coloured lad in an Armani baseball cap. We went straight for each other. More Plymouth piled out and both crews faced off in the road outside the pub. Steve and his brother from Port Talbot rushed past me into a couple of Plymouth. "Soul Crew! Soul Crew!" We had the first lot of Plymouth on the back step but had to battle like hell as they kept coming back with more numbers. People were floored from both sides.

It was Titch's twenty-first birthday and he was clearly enjoying himself. We were now in the middle, virtually holding each other together. "Fucking keep it together," people screamed at each other. For a second it seemed we were done for as the locals came in front, to the side and behind us from a park. We rallied and nearly everyone went in again. Then we started to get the upper hand and could see more of them on the floor than us. As the fighting spilled into the park, their confidence began to go.

Most fights at football last a minute or two at most but this was 15 minutes at least before the police arrived. It was nuts. I had blood all down my new yellow Stone Island coat but I don't think it was mine. Everyone was knackered and finally the police turned up heavily and with dogs. As the fists and boots kept flying, the truncheons started flying too. Within seconds the mobs were separated for the first time in what seemed ages.

One Plymouth lad, who we nickname Pinkie, stood out from the rest. He took a big beating but still came back mouthing. The police tried to shut him up but he wouldn't give in. He was covered in blood and cuts. "We thought you were the best in the country," he screamed.

"We are," I replied, as he got whacked to the floor with a cracking right hander from Nobby.

Plymouth's firm were all now in the park. It's not always easy to estimate numbers but I reckon they had 120 to our 30. A couple of our boys got nicked and the police watched in wonder as we started clapping each other, shaking each others' hands and hugging. Immediately we made up a song about our day, which we sang to them: "Outnumbered three to one, we had Plymouth on the run." It may be a tad childish but everyone was buzzing. Later Plymouth said it was the gamest little firm they have ever seen.

We were escorted to the ground, every one of us being filmed. A few swapped caps and jackets in a vain attempt to stay inconspicuous. We paid in and all the Central Element were to our right in the seats. There were around 200 Cardiff fans there and the stories about our battle began. Some boys swore we were fighting for half an hour. I don't think we were but it did feel like it. The police then came in pointing people out. I was surprised that we didn't all get nicked.

Everyone was in an excellent mood and Cardiff went on to win 2-1. I taped the goals on telly just so I could replay our mob going ballistic when we scored. Nothing beats a good goal celebration, the madder the better. On leaving the ground we met Stevie Weasel, who hadn't bothered going to the game. He had walked to the Plymouth end and been jumped by five Plymouth but fought back and they left him, respecting his gameness. The police had found our driver in town and made him bring the coach to the ground. The driver was baffled. He said the police had told him we were all violent soccer thugs and had been involved in a serious outbreak of disorder. "I can't believe it," he said, "all such nice boys, well-dressed in your shirts and jackets." He told us he'd had more bother on his coach taking drunken rugby fans on tour. We were escorted out of town.

Some of the lads were charged with various offences after that fight. One book I've read mentions that Plymouth waited for Cardiff at the court to take them for a drink as a mark of respect. This is true. Ten Plymouth were outside and took a couple of lads for a beer. Some people never understood how you could talk to rival lads, but why not? To be feared and respected was what I wanted for Cardiff. I think after that day Plymouth felt both for us. The feeling was mutual. As the Plymouth-Cardiff saga continued, Cardiff showed their respect by turning up at every opportunity.

The season after, we had another coach with virtually the same people on board. An idea that had been discussed for months was to go to the Britannia pub before them – to sit in there from opening time and show them that the previous season had been no fluke. We picked up in Cardiff at 7am: different driver but same old lies, the shopping trip routine. You won't believe how big a nightmare it is to get a private coach for the football, nearly impossible. Anyway, the journey was bad news from the off. A police van with a cameraman started tailing us. Other Cardiff were due to meet us in the

Britannia, many of them who had missed the first one no doubt sick of hearing about "Plymouth" this and "Plymouth" that, but now I had a feeling it wasn't going to be the same. This police van tailed us until we turned into a service station. Then the driver told us that there was something wrong with the coach. It all seemed strange, or was I being paranoid?

As we approached Plymouth some time later, two police vans came up alongside and a police bike drove in front, indicating to our driver to make a left into a long side road. We turned a corner past a Little Chef, and Wasp suddenly shouted, "What the fuck?" There on the lay-by were around 50 officers on foot, half a dozen vans, bikes and dogs. The works. "I don't think we're going to the Britannia today boys," someone piped up. Too fucking right. It seemed the whole of the Devon police force was there to greet us.

The driver did as he was told and got off the bus. Then officer after officer boarded, moving towards the back of the bus until they filled the aisle. One at a time we were taken off the coach, searched, handcuffed and put into prison vans with separate compartments. It took them a while to search us all. I was pissed off that Plymouth weren't going to see our firm. I really didn't give a monkey's where they were taking us. We were all then driven away.

We had been arrested under the new law, prevention of breach of the peace, where if they feel they have a valid enough reason they will arrest you before anything happens. It's a liberty really. We were told afterwards that we were the first group of football fans in the country to suffer such fate. We were taken to three different nicks: Plymouth, Torquay and Exeter. I ended up in Torquay with around ten of the others. We weren't even interviewed, just arrested and bunged in cells. After a while they let us into the yard for a kickabout with a ball and let us listen to the football on Radio 5 Live. They were decent to us, which was something. One of them even went to a shop to get us some Torquay rock.

They released us at 7.30pm, well after the end of the game, and gave the coach a further escort to pick up all our other boys. We could now speak on the mobiles to the Cardiff who had actually got to the ground and one boy told us the Central Element had 100 waiting but the locals knew what had happened to us. I've seen some police escorts in my time but this one took the biscuit. They escorted us every mile to Cardiff, only turning back at Cardiff Castle.

The Plymouth rivalry entered the next season. The away game was not long before Christmas and a no-no for most of the lads. After the match, eight Cardiff on their way back to their van were ambushed by 50 Plymouth. One of our best-known faces, Neath Punk, was there. Firstly some Plymouth approached him and asked, "Where's your firm?" He is basically known not to give a fuck and said, "Here we are," and whacked the lad in the face, only to be jumped on by loads of Plymouth. He suffered three broken ribs after a nasty kicking but took it as an occupational hazard. It wound me up to hear about it – what is the point of 50 attacking eight?

It added an element of revenge when the Central Element came to South Wales at the end of the season. A couple of our lads had been speaking to them and they promised to come early. Such rumours are rife but this one proved true. By midday, 100-plus Cardiff were ready at one of our favourite old downtown pubs. TCE were in touch. They were told in no uncertain terms to head for town. Some people wanted to move but others told them to stay patient, and word duly came back that they had been spotted up near the ground. Why had they gone there? There was nothing for it but to march the firm from town up into Canton, the area where the ground is located.

Everyone wanted this badly for Neath Punk. "Come on Cardiff, you lazy bastards, keep up," the frontrunners yelled, as some were strolling. As Cardiff turned the corner up towards the Ninian pub, Jonny and Mark T from the Docks got out of their car and said 40 Plymouth had parked outside the ground and made their way to the pub. Jeff, a well-known copper in the city, was heard to warn the Plymouth not to go to the Ninian for their own safety but they ignored him. Most of them were standing outside the pub as Cardiff got close.

As we got down towards the pub a few Plymouth spotted us. They threw some bottles as we sprinted towards them, and I do mean sprinted. About 25 of them were outside and started to back off straight away. Ricky from Roath and another lad were already in the pub and kicked off. We got up close and caught three or four of them, who got hammered on the floor. The rest ran. They turned and tried to make a stand but had such a torrid time that they ended up being chased all the way to the Grange End, where the police barricaded them and saved them. That's one hell of a distance to get kicked and punched. Needless to say, Neath Punk was right at the front gaining revenge. Maybe ten Plymouth were bloodied, with two lying unconscious as we made our way back to the pub. Six Plymouth later had to be taken to hospital for treatment.

On the way back to the pub, more Plymouth were run and two were spotted still in the Ninian, frozen to the spot. Some Cardiff wanted them butchered but one of our good lads, started to chat to them to put them at ease. He then told them to come with him and walked them to the ground, through hundreds of Cardiff still hanging around. He got them to the safety of the Grange End and they hugged him like he had saved their lives. They told him it was the most scared they have ever been. It was the proper thing to do, to leave them alone. Jeff the copper later was heard to tell the Plymouth firm, "I don't want to say I told you so."

After the game, most of the boys disappeared but in the evening we heard that the Plymouth, having picked up their mates from hospital, had set their sights on a hit-and-run and attacked a pub with only a few Cardiff in. Word flashed round that their buses were parked near the ice rink. Around 15 older Cardiff heads from Ely and Canton got together, found them and chased them back to their buses. They ended up driving the wrong way up the road. Every window on the two buses was trashed. I later spoke to some Plymouth and they told me they had to drive home without any windows, all covered in blood, getting laughed at by motorists driving by. Plymouth are held in fair esteem by Cardiff but they would be first to admit they were out of their league that sunny April in South Wales.

A week later, four of us went to Maine Road to see an Oasis gig. In the morning, Manchester United were playing Nottingham Forest at Old Trafford, so we went for a nose. Outside Lou Macari's chip shop, we saw three Plymouth, there for the same reason as us. We went for a drink and they told us it was the worst time they had ever had. They also thanked us that no knives were used on the lads who were grounded. I told them even though a lot of firms do still "carry" (weapons), Cardiff would never do that.

Over the past few years the police have been the winner with this fixture.

CHAPTER EIGHTEEN

Yorkshire Men

VISITING A NEW stadium is always an attraction and in the 1995-96 season we had our first trip to the McAlpine in Huddersfield. At the time, City were languishing near the bottom of Division Two (surprise, surprise) but I was still keen to make the trip. I ended up going with some lads from a little village about ten miles from Cardiff: 12 of us in a minibus. Cardiff had had a run-in with Huddersfield in the 1980s. I had been to their old ground when I was 17; we won 3-2 with only about 100 Cardiff fans there and I was on telly, celebrating like an idiot. I had also become good friends with a Huddersfield lad who was seeing a girl who followed Cardiff. Though he was Everton through and through, he drank with Town's firm and if they were involved in any decent games, or battles, I'd find out straight away. He was my voice of the north, so to speak.

We were due to meet other City once we reached Huddersfield but this was one of those times when our following wasn't up to much. As we drove past the train station, we saw the lad I knew, who was on his way to watch Everton. Our driver shouted him and he came over sheepishly, then perked up when he realised it was someone he knew. We asked him where we could get a drink. He told us Huddersfield were turning out a big mob today and for us to keep away from the Crescent with what we had. We didn't give a fuck how many locals were turning out as long as the other City showed: at least ten more and I'd be happy. But what can you expect to do with a dozen in places like this? We parked and walked down the hill into the town centre. On the corner is the George Hotel and over the road about 100 yards away is the Crescent. We decided to go into the hotel, which had a large bar and lounge. It was a fairly posh place but no-one was wearing any colours and we all looked relatively smart. The staff greeted us warmly. As time wore on we could see lads passing outside, making their way to the Crescent, which was clearly visible from the George windows.

One lad came in, surveying the pub, and walked up to me. I had a red Paul and Shark pullover on.

"Nice jumper mate," he said.

"Cheers."

He asked where I got it from and I told him London. After a short pause he said in a broad Yorkshire accent, "Are you lot Cardiff?"

"Yeah we are."

"How many of you is there?"

I told him that only our minibus was here. He had a look around, said goodbye and left. I had a feeling it wouldn't be long before some more checked us out. Right on cue, they came in. A couple of them knew the Everton lad well and we chatted. There was a big coloured lad there who runs with Man City. I had heard about him previously. He came over.

"Is there more coming or what?"

"No, I think this is it now for the day."

I think we started hinting that we were only there now for a drink. One said, "You fucking terrorised Bradford, didn't you, your lot? How come you've not brought a big firm here?" Despite the surface banter, a couple of them were clearly itching for us to have a pop but we did nothing. Eventually they left, leaving one lad on his own. "There's enough of you here now, isn't there?" he kept saying. It was obvious we were about to see the local mob in full flow.

The 12 of us knew trouble was around the corner, literally, but we decided to stay. Inside we were all thinking, *fuck*, but no way would we show it. *We are Cardiff*, and all that. Minutes later we could see from the window that the Crescent was emptying. Lads were coming out adjusting their caps and gloves. All the Huddersfield firm were now across the road, facing the pub. We got up and a couple of the boys grabbed stools. The staff started to panic.

About 20 Huddersfield came to the door. "Come on you Welsh bastards." We did nothing. There was a lot of goading and hand-waving but we stood there smiling. The manager appeared with a key and rushed to lock the door. There were now 50 outside, at least. I honestly thought we had no chance but these lads I was with wouldn't back down from anyone and I didn't feel worried at all. These boys were older Cardiff fans from the same village and would virtually die for each other.

The pub manager made a comment about the local mob being a bunch of bullies. We told him that, many times, if we travelled in small numbers we would find much larger gangs suddenly getting brave and wanting to have a pop. I was thinking that if a good 50 of us were there they wouldn't have even come out of the pub. Anyway the police arrived soon after and an officer came in, had a look around and then asked us how we had got there. We told him our minibus was outside the station. He made the driver walk up there with an officer and bring it outside the hotel so they could escort us to the ground. The locals were still mingling outside the hotel and at this point I felt embarrassed, even though we were severely outnumbered.

Two officers were present and they led us towards our minibus. By now the Huddersfield mob was around 60 strong and congregated over the road. Before we got into the bus, some of them started wolf-whistling and cheering, really taking the piss. It was the straw that broke the camel's back. I watched in amazement as one of our lads, Hally, lost his head, charged around and ran straight into the middle of the road. *What the fuck was he doing?* The locals came rushing over and he went toe-to-toe with the first one. We had to help him and we all got stuck in behind him. They were swarming all over us but, just like the first time at Plymouth, we were all together to a man, punching and kicking, and a big gap opened up. I think they were shocked more than anything. They then seemed to come in one at a time. This was easy for Rhysey, one of the toughest lads there. It was like a Bruce Lee film: he floored them one after another. They kept coming and forced us back onto the pavement, where we literally had our backs to the wall. The two coppers were trying their utmost to keep us apart but Huddersfield now were getting right on top of us.

Outside the hotel was a sandwich board. Hally managed to grab it and launched it into a cluster of Huddersfield, which backed them off. This was our only chance. We steamed back into the road and for a few sweet seconds I couldn't believe it, they were taking a back step. He picked up the sandwich board again and launched it, again. Now we had them back on the other side of the road, every one to a man going in the wrong direction. Police reinforcements arrived and blocked our way in the middle of the road. The pandemonium was over.

What a buzz. We should by rights have all been lying on the floor. Some police held us against the wall while others chased off the locals. After some discussion, we were put back in the minibus. Some of the locals made a half-hearted attempt to have another go but all they got out of us was a chant of "Shit, shit, shit." In the bus we were buzzing. I couldn't wait to get to the ground to tell the others what they had missed but the police van kept escorting us, we thought to the ground. We should have thought again.

We were taken straight to the police station and banged up in cells. They didn't nick any of their lot, just us. At about

10pm we were all let out. They charged a lot of us with affray, which, if proved in court, could mean a heavy sentence. Our main worry was that they had filmed the fight but it turned out it hadn't. The statements from the officers were accurate: that 12 Welshmen charged against the 60 Huddersfield. In the end the charges were dropped to public order and we were bound over for a year. After travelling up there for the sentencing, we had a look at the shops in Leeds and then went back to Huddersfield for a celebratory drink. Yes, you've guessed it, to the Crescent. There was nobody about but we had a chat with the decent landlord. I have since bumped into a few Huddersfield on different occasions. They have quite a decent rep hooligan-wise but won't forget the dozen hardy Welsh souls that day.

ANOTHER RUN-IN WITH a Yorkshire club in the 1990s took place with Bradford City. In the 1980s Cardiff had turned up in Bradford in massive numbers, but they never reciprocated by bringing a crew across the Welsh border until 1994. That year we played them at home before Christmas. They were known to have a tight, violent crew called the Ointment. We met in the Owain in town at around noon. Seven or eight of us sat around suffering the after-effects of partying all night at Spice of Life at Cardiff University, where the hippest clubbers would dance side by side with a bunch of hooligans. While we were paying the price of too much fun, one of the Ely lads came up and told us that there were 50 lads walking around town. No one really took much notice. *Bradford won't come here*, I thought. How wrong I was. As I ordered a drink at the bar, the doors opened and in they came, one after another, all shapes and sizes and with a few different races too. The had some big bastards and they surrounded us. We were stuck.

"Go get your riot gear on lads, the Ointment's here," said one of their blacks.

"Give us a bit and well get our mob back here," replied
Stevie Weasel. He was immediately punched in the side of the
face. This was heavy. With little choice, we all made our way
out. Then Neath Punk and Matty, two of our crazies, yelled,
"Fuck 'em. Come on, let's have you outside!"

I thought, *What the fuck are you doing, shut up*. It was bad
enough that we were so outnumbered and being forced to
leave but I was on a comedown too. They didn't follow us and
we managed to escape fairly intact.

Next thing we had to do was to get the lads. No way could
Bradford get away with this. I wouldn't have been able to
sleep. We went to the usual haunts closer to the ground and
within the hour had raised a good 35. We caught the bus back
into town. We were spitting. *The cheeky bastards,* I was
thinking. There was no sign of the police so we made our way
off the bus and quickly to the Owain. We burst through the
doors. They had gone. Why didn't they wait, we said we'd
come back? No-one knew where they were until we heard that
they had walked past the Ninian Pub in an escort but some
had got free and been decked. That was scant consolation.
After the game we had 60 together – Docks, Ely, Roath and a
few Valleys – but they were long gone. Well, they hadn't seen
the last of us.

As fate would have it the return fixture was on the final day
of the season. Cardiff were already relegated but always make
the last game a bit of an occasion. We knew the police would
be out in force, so the Soul Crew would have to try something
a bit special to get around them. Our last home game – a
spectacular 7-2 defeat by Cambridge – was an opportunity to
sort out names and deposits. Someone booked two late coaches
from a luxury holiday firm, telling them it was for a wedding
reception in Halifax. There were 110 lads on these buses from
all over South Wales: it was the cream of the Soul Crew.

None of us wore club colours but it didn't take the driver
long to suss that we weren't going to a wedding party. Still,

we arrived in Halifax undetected by the local plod. Another City coach was there, most of them enjoying a good drink. We were there for something different: we had a score to settle.

We took the train from Halifax station for the short trip to Bradford, only to run into Cardiff police there with the local bobbies. Shakespeare from NCIS was there too and was flapping straight away as soon as he saw me. "Here they are, these are ours," said the Cardiff cops but there weren't enough officers there to do much and we marched straight past, down the steps and into the city centre. Often our organisation was poor but today it was spot on.

Outside the station was a pub called the Queen's where Bradford were supposed to be. The doors were locked and the curtains drawn. We got to the edge of the shopping area and waited for everyone to regroup. A broad coloured lad came over.

"Where's the Ointment?" one of the lads asked.

"Fuckin' 'ell," he replied, "this is a bad firm, man. I'll take you to them."

We all started following our new friend. He kept on saying about this being the best crew he had seen in Bradford since Sheffield United in the early 1980s. We had lost the police and made our way through some pedestrianised streets. There were pockets of two and three lads scattered about but they'd scarper if we got too close. Not that we'd touch them anyway; we weren't Jacks. This was the Soul Crew. He took us up a hill and two bottles of Bud came flying through the air at us. We got to the top of the hill and on the left stood the Market Tavern pub. Around 30 Ointment were on other side of the road and we ran straight over to them. They didn't stand for a second. One small lad with blond hair came to the door of the pub, saw us, and ran back in. Another came out and fired a flare gun. Most of us ducked to the floor and the flare whizzed off harmlessly. We charged to the doors.

Mark H, Jonny and Richard from the Docks went straight in the pub. Bradford were already running down stairs into what I think were living quarters. There must have been 50 of them inside and they were all trying to flee. It was two minutes of utter chaos. Table and stools were used to annihilate the locals. Most of them got out of a back door and some downstairs but a few were left cowering on the floor.

Police moved into the pub and started beating us out of the place. As we left I noticed that every window had been smashed. I hadn't even noticed them getting broken. The police then herded us around the corner as they tried to get reinforcements. We were finally rounded up and some locals made an attempt to have a go. They were laughed off. Our police arrived on the scene with Shaky, the football intelligence officer, who loved a bit of cat and mouse. I remember copper Jeff shaking his head a couple of times and seeming to have a little grin to himself.

We were kept outside a shop in a busy street for about 20 minutes. Some Bradford came close; it was some of the ones who had been legged earlier and a few I recognised from the Cardiff game. We had a good giggle at them. The new line of Burberry checked shirts had only a few days earlier arrived on the shelves in London. I had one on underneath my Lacoste coat but some northern copper had to make sure he ripped it for me. Thanks. We were taken to the ground. Some locals followed the escort but I think they realised they weren't dealing with an ordinary firm, judging by the looks on their faces.

The away seats were packed with 2,500 Cardiff. Bradford, who were in the play-offs, attracted quite a large gate and their firm sat in their stand to our left. There were also a couple of Cardiff mingled in unnoticed, which is often the case when we have a decent-sized following. The last game brings out all sorts, including the fancy dress brigade, and always reminds me of Birmingham when their mob rioted at Crystal Palace, many of then in clown, Nazi and Batman clobber. Predictably we lost the game 2-0.

We came out into an alleyway, which was on a slope. At the top of the alley was the road where Bradford would head after leaving their seats. The police tried to push us back but 50 or so got through. We got to the top road and it was full of Bradford. Some Cardiff started barging through, then a big group of dressers passed. Fair play to them, they came steaming into us and it was proper off again, both sides not giving an inch. Two policemen on horseback charged between us, forcing us back down the small alley. From behind us bollards were thrown at the police as more Cardiff came up the alley. Bradford retreated for a second but it was even on that road. The police then forced us down the alley and escorted 150 of us back to the station.

Some Bradford were in the Queen's, with others on the pavement outside. Neath Punk walked straight towards them. He wore this big leather coat with a massive furry collar and looked nuts. He went into the middle of three or four or them and in a broad West-Walian accent shouted, "Come to Halifax if you want another beating." These Bradford looked horrified.

Halifax was swarming with police. We had planned to stay till late but the local bobbies had other ideas. They were okay with us though and let the boys have an hour in the pub before we had to make our way home. At the start of the next season, one of our boys was taken to one side on a train back for a London game by one of Cardiff's many football coppers. This copper declared how genuinely impressed they were with what was done at Bradford. "Ten out of ten for everything" were his words. They obviously have their job to do but most police who work closely and regularly with soccer firms do, I feel, build up a certain amount of mutual respect. The papers, on the other hand, condemned the behaviour

and a Bradford spokesman even labelled all Cardiff fans
hooligans. For the Soul Crew, the moral of the story was
simple: Don't mess with Cardiff.

CHAPTER NINETEEN

Crossing Swords

IN A DECADE with the Soul Crew, I crossed swords with many different football firms. The ones that gave the most trouble were not always those you would expect. All boys know and respect the likes of the ICF, the Zulus, the 6.57 and the Middlesbrough Frontline, but there other tight-knit little mobs that can give you the shock of your life if you underestimate them.

The first experience I had with Wrexham came in the 1988-89 season, when they played Hereford United in the Welsh Cup final. English border teams such as Hereford were allowed in the competition in those days. As the game would be played at the national stadium in our beloved capital city on a beautiful Sunday afternoon, it was guaranteed the Soul Crew would be represented. Until that day the stories I had heard about the Wrexham Front Line Crew were limited. They'd never really been rivals with Cardiff, despite a few skirmishes here and there. Their fans were well into following Wales and a group or two could always be seen at international games, no matter how bad Wales were doing.

The morning of the game saw some Wrexham and Hereford come to blows in the Canal Boat pub on the edge of the city. Cardiff met at Central Hotel by Mill Lane. Word soon spread that 100-plus Wrexham were drinking by the castle. One of the Docks boys made a move to Wrexham to let them know the score. By 1pm I was among up to 40 Cardiff, mainly

Docks lads, who had gathered. It was a scorcher of a day, so most of us stood outside. The police then were very low-key so it looked like a good opportunity for something to happen. Some Cardiff were on the other side of St Mary's Street, looking down Caroline Street. Jonny from the Docks, who had been chatting to Wrexham, came back. They knew where we were by now.

It was 2.30 when the shouts came up. A mob appeared out of Caroline Street and onto St Mary's Street, about 70 yards from us, and turned left towards us. They looked the part and certainly had the numbers. My heart was pounding. I knew I was with good lads but to be honest I was a bit nervous. They put a jog on towards us. The first 20 or so Wrexham jumped over the barriers into the central reservation, got to about 30 yards away and stopped. A couple had their arms wide open. Cardiff just walked out to meet them. The first four or five Cardiff out were black, which for whatever reason many white lads find intimidating. After the initial walk the 40 of us just ran straight towards Wrexham. One punch later and a bottle thrown and they were running. I could not believe my eyes. Some were chased down Caroline Street (*aka* Chip Alley). I later heard their excuses, saying they had too many young lads with them, but it was a disastrous day for the Front Line.

In 1991, Wales had Belgium away in Brussels in a European Championship qualifier, to be played in Anderlecht Stadium, a few miles from the centre. The main bulk of Cardiff booked to travel on the Sunday evening. Two nights earlier, we played at Wrexham in a mid-table Division Two game. Around 200 Cardiff made the trip, with a sprinkling of boys. We had a minibus just from Aberdare. We got to Wrexham right on kick-off and stood on the old terrace, beneath the seats behind the goal. To our left sat 25-30 lads of all ages, dressed in Soviet and Berghaus, the big labels in the north for a while. We just stood there and smiled as they immediately clocked us. I happened to have a red Stone Island three-quarter duffel coat on, which wasn't the least bit conspicuous. The mouthing to and fro soon started. Big Jason from Porthcawl and a minibus-full were telling us how they had it with this Wrexham mob outside the Turf pub, next to the ground. His shirt had been ripped to shreds and was in his pocket.

One of the Wrexham mob was a ginger, balding lad who had his eye on my coat. He would later become a close mate but at half-time he came to the seats with others, calling over in their Scouse-type accents, "You're fuckin' having it in Belgium." After the game the local plod put us back on the bus and we got home safely (with expensive coats intact).

On the Sunday, the Belgium-bound Cardiff contingent met up at Victoria station in London. This was a huge game for Wales and there must have been 150 of Cardiff's firm in Victoria, which we knew was one of Chelsea's favourite drinking haunts. In one pub were five clearly-nervous Swansea. They were actually treated well. The train journey to Dover was eventful, with lights and furniture getting destroyed by some extremely drunken members of the trip.

Once at the port, we waited in the ferry departure lounge. In walked five dressers who I recognised. They were well-known Swansea and obviously didn't suss some of the animals present. One Bridgend lad had a yellow Cardiff City top on and a Jack shouted, "What the fuck is that shit?" I thought I was hearing things: did he *really* just say that? He must have, for straight away they were surrounded. They were forced to sit down and one or two things were patiently explained to them. They suffered no physical violence but let's just say a certain amount of mental torture. They were made to carry an Ely Soul Crew flag and to have their photo taken with it – the photos are still about somewhere. They were also told that if they came on our ferry they would be going for a dip in the sea. I don't know whether the lads who made that threat were serious but the Swansea didn't board the ferry.

The crossing was a nightmare. Flash, my mate, got into a

terrible state after having too much to drink. He became extremely ill on board and would suffer all week. Once in Brussels we booked into hotels and then met up with other Valleys Cardiff. It was my first visit to Brussels and I really enjoyed it. The place had some decent clothes shops and a first-rate red light district. But by the Monday night it had gone off in the Grand Place, the focal point of Brussels. Two coaches of Front Line arrived and as they made their way to the hotel they asked a lad, "Where's Cardiff?" He immediately went to a nearby bar where a small group of Cardiff were. There were no more than 15 of them but they got up anyway. As soon as they saw each other it went off. Running battles ensued, even though the Wrexham still had their bags with them. It got pretty nasty at one stage, with a pub getting wrecked, and both sides present claimed victory. The police were soon on the scene and arrested lads from both clubs, with 80 Wrexham being detained and then deported. The next day we met the Cardiff in the Grand Place and listened to their stories. They were happy they had held their own with the numbers heavily against them.

The next time I saw Wrexham was a few months later in the Welsh Cup final. They played Swansea, once again in Cardiff. We had a decent little mob out waiting for Swansea but the Jacks never really came together. We slapped most of the ones we saw that morning. It was a pretty poor turnout from them for a Cup final. I was, however, to get to know the mouthy ginger skinhead a lot better. His name was Neil, and some months after Belgium I saw him with ten of his Front Line pals outside the away end before a game at Ninian Park. I went over to them and they asked how many Cardiff were out. "About ninety," I said. They asked how many Cardiff were going to a forthcoming Welsh game in Nuremberg. "About ninety," I said. The phrase stuck, and every time I saw them after that they would say, "Alright Ninety," which got to be my nickname with them on Welsh trips. That afternoon they were quite fortunate they didn't bump into the 90.

In January 1992, I went to the Wrexham vs Arsenal cup tie for a look, as Cardiff had been knocked out by the Jacks in the first round. I witnessed a small skirmish between them and Arsenal at the train station. Wrexham had about 150 and they looked decent lads. I was recognised by a couple outside the ground and spent the rest of the afternoon telling them about Cardiff's day in the FA Cup at Swansea. They must have thought I was exaggerating slightly about the turnout but have since seen our numbers over the years. Wrexham have always got lucky by playing big teams in the cups. They even got to play Man Utd in Europe. There is a legend that all Cardiff's cup ties are fixed, as we get poor draws all the time. The year we got to the fifth round we ended up with Luton Town, for heaven's sake.

The season we got promoted to Division Two, in 1993, we took over 4,000 to Wrexham with a couple of hundred in our mob. We made our way to Chester and went in by train, a wrong move, as the town centre is nigh on impossible to get to from the train station with a mob. Wrexham had a decent turnout in their seats but trouble was limited to the odd punch thrown here and there.

A couple of seasons later it was different: Cardiff vs Wrexham in the Welsh Cup final. The Front Line deserved every credit that day, even though they got run ragged after the game. They told Cardiff beforehand that they were parking in Newport and coming in on the train. They said they would be in early, asked us which was the best place to go, and went there. They were let down badly with the numbers but 40 of them turned up at 11.30 and went to the Central Hotel as arranged. About an hour later they burst out of the pub and around 100 Cardiff charged at them. Wrexham came out onto the road and stood for as long as they could before being forced to retreat to where some construction work was taking place. It was a bit crazy as they ended up being locked in a cage and were all huddled together being punched and kicked and couldn't do a thing about it. The police intervened and all this was caught on CCTV and led to severe jail sentences for six Cardiff fans. It also featured on a local documentary showing these Wrexham stuck in a cage. It looked bizarre.

After the game, which Wrexham won 2-1, the Front Line tried to walk back to the station – they had no chance. After being chased back in the ground, they were then kept, barricaded against a wall, protected by the police, for over an hour as around 300 Cardiff battled it out with the uniforms. But the lads took their hats off to Wrexham who I would even rate as the second best crew in Wales. No prizes for guessing who's first.

IN THE 1980s Newport County were respected by a lot of Cardiff. I had heard many tales of some good fisticuffs with Newport and a lot of the boys were disappointed when they went out of the Football League in the late '80s. They used to love the sly one though, trying to catch Cardiff unawares. I remember Cardiff playing Southend with not many lads out and 80 Newport turned up out of nowhere and smashed the pub up. Some of Cardiff's main lads also had some pretty personal encounters with the Newport lot. It got to a stage where people were going around to each other's houses, which is a tad over the top.

When Newport played Merthyr at Ninian Park in 1987, a small crew of Cardiff had a tough time of it (as Dave describes in Chapter Ten). I did manage to go to Somerton Park just before they knocked it down and Cardiff ran the County ragged. That season, their last in the league, they brought a decent mob to Cardiff and after the game they were brought up to the Ninian Park platform by mistake. A lot of the Valley Cardiff were there. A stand-off was broken up by the South Wales Old Bill forcing Newport back down the platform.

In 1991 they were drawn in Cardiff in the old Welsh Cup. It was chucking down, cold and dark. At about 6.30pm, 70 Newport came out of Central. Twenty-five of us left the pub, ran through the bus station and waited for the moment. It went swimmingly. They must have thought we had 100. We hit the front of their mob, they panicked and scarpered in all directions. They were fighting each other to get away. A couple got caught and got slapped on the floor but most disappeared.

I did bump into them again that evening though. My mate Flash and I were helping some girl who had a flat battery and had to push her car over the Taff Bridge by the Empire Pool. She thanked us and, as we walked off towards the ground, I looked around to see most of this County mob running towards us. The two of us sped off like rockets. The game had kicked off ages earlier but they had found the bottle to come back. I sprinted ahead and heard Flash – who obviously wasn't as quick as his nickname suggested – shouting for me. Two of them had him on the floor. I ran back. "Come on you Newport cunts," I shouted, trying my best to look ferocious. As they looked up, Flash wrestled his way to freedom, thankfully. I would never leave a friend but I'm glad he broke free – phew.

Another encounter with the Newport was at Stone Roses "Second Coming" gig at the Newport Centre in the mid-90s. Around 40 of us were lucky enough to get tickets and arrived at the venue for the gig. Above the main crowd was a seated area where we congregated in a party atmosphere, watching my favourite band of the decade before a full house.

Just before the end, somebody threw a Cardiff away jersey onto the stage. Ian Brown, the lead singer, took off his shirt to wear the Cardiff top. "Bluebirds, Bluebirds," was chanted all over the venue. That was the cue for some Newport to come over and sit among us. I think they were trying to look tough. They were given short shrift and told to get their boys together. At the end of an excellent show we moved out of the arena.

Around 30 locals were milling around the tee-shirt and poster sellers and three of them came over.

"Who the fuck are you?" Blondie asked.

"Who the fuck do you think we are?" one replied.

Crack – he was smashed in the jaw and it started. Posters went flying in the air and the crowd scattered as for five minutes we battered Newport. Some of them were game but it was 40 of our best and most of them ended back up in the foyer. Around five Newport stood as long as they could until the security dragged them in. Some took a real hiding and there was a bit of blood spilt. A big, bald lad with a Villa badge on was one of those brick walls. He got knocked down, punched and kicked all over the pavement but he still got up, shouting that he was Newport. Fair play to him. The *New Musical Express* among others reported the trouble, claiming it was Cardiff and Swansea. There were no Swansea present; none of them would have been cultured enough to attend a Roses gig.

The band that came off the back of the Stone Roses was of course Oasis and, thanks to one of our Wigan chums, some of mine and Dave's most surreal moments of the '90s were spent in their company. One of the Wiganers designed all the record covers for Oasis and The Verve, among others. I had seen them twice in Cardiff before meeting them: at the university in front of maybe 300 people and then Astoria on Queen Street a couple of years later where they got bottled off stage. They became huge in the mid-90s and played the CIA twice in 1996 and twice in 1998.

The Wigan lads had many a tale to tell about Liam. Every time we went out with them, his brother Noel seemed to be surrounded by politics and was rarely seen. But Liam, Meg Matthews and others were up for the party and due to the generous nature of the Wiganers it was VIP passes all round for us. Liam was surprisingly removed from his pompous, arrogant media portrayal and had loads of time for us. All the rumours of cocaine binges and excessive drinking among rock stars are purely fabricated!

One night, myself, Dave and Darren were in a room at Jury's, maybe around 4am, having a smoke trying to recover when in burst Liam Gallagher with more champagne. He sat on the edge of the bed I was lying on. Perhaps he had just come from a session with a groupie, as his shirt was undone and he looked particularly disheveled. The hotel radio played "Don't Look Back in Anger" and we watched in fascination as he started singing the song and sharing his champagne with us. Surreal. I think Dave said to him, "They play any shit on the radio nowadays, don't they?"

Another time my mate Steve from Aberdare couldn't make an after-show party. I had Liam phoning Steve, demanding he turned up. How could Steve go into work the day after and tell people, "Oh, Liam Gallagher phoned me last night asking me to go to a party"? This was all at the height of their fame. We have plenty of great memories from those times. I think the Wiganers still keep in touch with them but not as much now they have become family men.

OTHER SMALL MOBS would occasionally turn up in Cardiff to chance their arm. Oxford United once brought 40 lads and were in the Philharmonic pub by 11am but then to "avoid" detection put a massive Red Hand of Ulster flag in the window. Very clever. The police escorted them to the ground and we laughed as Oxford were clearly scared as they walked past 150 of us. Some of us even got in their escort, which horrified them. We returned the favour up there, with interest.

Stockport County who I had seen get legged by Cardiff up there, turned up with 30 once, giving it the mouth. They weren't mouthing for long and the ones who didn't end up doing some middle distance running ended up in the infirmary. Hereford United always used to be game for a laugh and did

turn up once or twice in Cardiff but always made sure they
had the police with them. One fight I remember with Hereford
was in pleasant surroundings of the Cathedral grounds at
their place in 1990. We chased them off, my flares flapping in
the wind. In '92 we had a bit of a decent run in the league and
we took 5,000 there. The poor bastards got swamped but still
made a bit of a stand.

One of the most violent incidents I have been involved in
was against a much bigger club: Celtic. In the mid-90s, Celtic
were drawn to play non-league Inter Cardiff in the UEFA
cup. Only a pocket of us turned out. Celtic, who have one of
the largest fan bases in the world, brought thousands but
maybe only 60 dressers. They drank in town all day and then
attacked us in the Borough, our pub, before we chased them
back to the Owain. The police got on the scene but 30 of us
got away and walked down Westgate Street towards the castle.
Some Celtic casuals came running up the road, soon followed
by the green-and-white-hooped brigade. There were 70 of
them at least, charging towards us, chanting, "Celtic". Loads
of them threw bottles. I am sure they thought we were going
to run off.

"Just spread across the road," one of us said.

The first Celtic came towards me and I said, "We ain't
going nowhere." Neath Punk, as usual, ran in and hit the
first one. I followed and whacked the next casual on his arse.
We steamed them: as soon as they had thrown their bottles,
the Celtic shirts didn't know what to do. We were backing
them off all the way down Westgate Street. It was superb.
There were about 20 casuals with them who did try to stand,
before five police vans came speeding down the road towards
us. Everyone scarpered in different directions as the police
tried to grab some of us. Most got away. We got together
again, now on a high, and decided to walk to the Ninian to
have a go at a lot of them. This 30 wouldn't budge from
anyone and we were pretty confident. On the way we chased

loads of shirters. We knew the closer we got to the ground, the tougher it was going to become but we weren't bothered. The Ninian was heaving, with the bar and the lounge full of Celtic.

"Lets do it then," we said. We swaggered in and a song went up, "No surrender, no surrender, no surrender to the IRA." Before I carry on, one or two Cardiff have strong views on Ulster and the loyalist thing but most couldn't care less. Personally, I have never been strongly motivated by politics, race or religion. If a football lad is black, white or yellow, if he's part of the mob that's all that matters. It was sung just to wind them up and it worked. The doors flew open and we were stuck in the passageway and showered with, I reckon, every bottle and glass in the pub. It was that bad I thought somebody could die. We tried to grab a few of them through the doors but the bombardment of glass was non-stop and we couldn't do much about it. For a second there was nothing being thrown and we tried to rush into the bar. We caught some Celtic in the doorway in a vicious fight. A police van turned up and gas was sprayed. At first we didn't know whether it was sprayed by Celtic or the police. We left the pub as police tried to restore order. There was blood everywhere. Three of our lot ended up in hospital due to the cuts from the glass. It was five minutes of mayhem.

We got together outside and attacked any Celtic fans in groups that we saw. Their shirts are just as mad as their casuals, no doubt, if provoked. After the game there were a few skirmishes but Celtic dispersed pretty quickly. As four of us walked back to our car in Canton at around 11pm we walked past four Celtic on the Taff Bridge. We ran at them and they legged it but we caught one. We didn't hurt him physically but we were cruel. We all held on to him and hung him over the bridge just by his trainers until he started to cry. Looking back, it was a shitty thing to do but it seemed funny at the time. We brought him back up and let him go and as he ran off, he turned and shouted, "Fuck you, you bastards." So he was okay.

Another Scottish side to turn up in Wales was Aberdeen, who played at Barry Town in a European game. A handful of Cardiff went there. I missed the fight, in the early evening, when six Aberdeen ended up in hospital after 40 of them were attacked by ten Barry Nutty Locals, one with a hammer, who took pleasure in smashing the Jocks over the head with it as they were stuck in the doorway of a pub trying to get out. After the game a couple more Aberdeen got smacked. I don't think they enjoyed their time in Wales at all. Antwerp of Belgium also brought a good 50 casuals once, stood for a while but eventually ran off. A couple have been back a few times and are fairly decent lads.

A MOB THAT deserves a little mention is Doncaster Rovers. They actually came to us in 1991. A few of us were queuing to get in the ground when some lads came behind us and one shouted in a strong Yorkshire accent, "Do you want it or what lads?" We looked around stunned and went towards him and they straight away shot off. We followed and saw about 25 of them behind a police line queuing to go in the away end seats. We told as many people as we could in the Bob Bank and after the game 20 of us waited in the car park to see how they had got there. As they came out, we were surrounded by our local police spotters. They kept us penned in and all we could do was watch these Doncaster pass. Their 25 was a good little number to travel that far for a club as small as them but of course we had to give them a welcome in the hillsides.

As it happened they had two cars parked near the Ninian but we learned the rest were on the train. The two cars disappeared but ten of us took taxis to Cardiff Central. A couple of us walked in the concourse to see what the police situation was. There weren't any. One of the Doncaster lads spotted us and ran up the stairs to the platform. We immediately followed. I give them credit, they came charging down the stairs at us with bins. They didn't know how many we had but they still took the fight to us. One bin hit me in the shoulder and it hurt: one of those big metal ones. For a minute we were just shouting at each other until one of them said, "C'mon Cardiff, you can't even do Donny." As he said that, three Cardiff came from behind them, so they were in the middle. We steamed in from both sides and they lost their bottle and scattered. We hit them all over the platform, two of them running onto the track. I remember one woman screaming, "Help him, help him," as we gave one a hammering on the floor. "They're going to kill him," she cried. We moved a bit sharpish out of the station but we spoke about the Donny after, admiring their guts.

For the return game 50 of us travelled on an early train. We were in Doncaster by noon but there was no sign of them. We spoke to a few in the ground, one asking about our Stone Island jackets. On another occasion some of us went up to Doncaster after we won promotion at Scunthorpe. There were running battles for ages. We came out on top but they still give us a run for our money. Some of their town lads are the Donny Whites, a big part of the Leeds Service Crew. I know good mobs like Pompey, Wolves and Hull have come unstuck against Doncaster.

I HAD FIRST seen Burnley at Turf Moor in the last game of the season in 1988. I had just turned 16 and we had secured promotion from the old Division Four along with Wolves. Cardiff took 4,000 up to Lancashire and battled in the streets all afternoon. At the game a Cardiff fan got stabbed and the locals to our left held up his blood-stained shirt. Cardiff ended up fighting with the police, Burnley came on the pitch, some Cardiff joined them and a little free-for-all occurred in the penalty area. Some Burnley I have later spoken to say this was one of the best crews they ever fought.

The season 1992 was pretty similar. Burnley were top of
the table in April and we were fourth. The local paper had a
field day, dubbing this the match of the season and stating
that Burnley would bring over 4,000 with them. The thought
of a massive away following really gets the Cardiff fans sitting
up and taking notice. In the end only 1,100 Burnley showed,
not really with a firm but loads of lads in vans. I think all of
them bar none got ambushed that day. Two vans down by St
David's Hospital in Canton were simply demolished. It was
the biggest home mob of Cardiff I had seen up until then and
Burnley were wise not to come in numbers. Just after kick-off
there was still over 100 of us hanging around. The crowd
touched 17,000, which for the Fourth Division was pretty
remarkable. A few vans turned up late and I asked them,
"Where have you been?" until I was dragged away by the
police. One Burnley lad opened the back doors of the van and
shouted to me, "I'll see you in two weeks." *Whatever*, I
thought. Cardiff lost 2-0 and after the game there was major
trouble with the police. I had my arse bitten by a police dog,
which ripped the pocket of my Armani jeans.

The build up to Burnley away included them threatening
the club. The *South Wales Echo* reported "Revenge will be
taken" after some of them had been hurt in Cardiff. As we
needed a miracle to reach the play-offs at that stage of the
season, the interest for Burnley away dwindled. Still, a few of
us jumped on a private coach from Cardiff. We got to Burnley
at around 4:30pm and nine of us got off. The rest for whatever
reason didn't want to join us. We knew we were up against it
but we went for it anyway. Myself, Abe, Jelly Legs, Matty,
Richy from Neath, Ricky and friend, Mal and someone else
who I can't remember walked straight into the town centre.

"It's fucking suicide this," I said to Matty.

"I know," he said, smiling.

The rest is all a bit hazy. I remember 30 men walking
around the corner and then running towards us. We just

charged at them only to halt in our tracks when one of our lot shouted, "Stop, they're Cardiff." They weren't Cardiff at all. Then rocks and bottles bounced off cars around us as the Burnley got closer. We backed off, then got run. I think we were screaming at each other to stand but it was too late. Apparently I ran down a dead end and took a pretty decent kicking, getting knocked unconscious. The boys found me later and sent for an ambulance.

I came around, half soaked, in hospital, to ask Matty, "Did we do 'em?" Matty denying any knowledge of what I meant, due to the police sitting next to us. He discharged me from the hospital even though I'm sure I was supposed to stay the night and we got to the ground in a taxi. Matty later told me that while he was carrying me into the ground I was further attacked by some Burnley locals. The stewards walked me across the side of pitch to the away end, to the delight of the Burnley fans. Afterwards I couldn't understand why they left a brand new £400 reflective Stone Island coat and stole an £8 Lacoste hat. Fair play to them though: I have had a few slaps along the way but this was a quality kicking. I was black and blue and aching for weeks. They ruined the jacket though, which is harder to get over than a broken nose. I couldn't wash the blood out. People who spoke to me in the ground that evening recall me thinking I was in Aberdare and stating that I had been attacked outside one of my local pubs. I think I was pretty concussed. I was helped on to the Valley Supporters' bus by Lee and Steve. I wouldn't have known what bus I came up on anyway.

The times Burnley have been due in Cardiff since, we have had huge turnouts but we have always been disappointed, though the Suicide Squad of Burnley are rated. Incidentally, I have seen written and heard said that the buzz of football violence is like sex. Well I'm sorry but I failed to see the connection that night between a large gang of northern boneheads taking turns to kick and thump me, and having sex. No similarity at all.

CHAPTER TWENTY

Having a Nose

BY THE MIDDLE of the 1990s I was so interested in hooliganism that I would often travel to see different clubs and check out their firms. I wasn't alone. Around the country was a small network of like-minded young men who did the same thing. It was almost a hobby, and I got to know people from many different areas and to spot familiar faces wherever I went.

One unmissable venture was England v Scotland at Euro 96. Wales had missed out on the tournament – yet again – but that wouldn't stop me from going to have a nose at what promised to be a major gathering of hooligan gangs. The hype in the press was unprecedented: the invasion of the tartan army, could the authorities handle the game, etc, etc.

I set off on the train. The dress at the time was Zegna cap, Iceberg History polo shirt, Paul Smith jeans, Adidas Trimm Trabb and the obligatory Cardiff pin badge. I met Scouse Steve, who lives and works in London. He is the most genuine person you will ever meet and definitely the most clued up on football and fashion. This guy will buy something and you know months later it is bound to catch on.

He had arranged to meet some mutual friends from Wigan in the Spread Eagle in Camden. It was a beautiful day and when we got there at 11am the Wiganers were outside on the benches. Also there were some Forest, Wolves and Derby, and with the Wigan lads was Richard Ashcroft of The Verve. He is obviously not a hooligan but was with one of the Wigan people who has an exceptional job in the music industry. Every time I have met these Wigan boys they have made me feel welcome. They are all clued-up, proper football lads. A couple were wearing Hilfiger on the day, two years before it came to Britain. They'd got it from New York and it wasn't long before I was out there buying some, but over the past couple of years it hasn't really caught on as it should have, the main reason being a flood of fake gear way before the good stuff was given a chance.

The police were out in force in Camden and came over to question everyone in and outside of the pub. One approached me and my Cardiff badge pretty much threw him. He asked what I was doing there. I explained that seeing as I followed Cardiff and Wales, my chances of visiting Wembley Stadium were remote, so I was going to take this chance to see the famous ground up close. I wasn't going to tell him that I had been there probably ten times before. I'm sure he didn't believe me anyway; he searched me, took my details and left. I told this story in the pub to the Wiganers and it made Richy Ashcroft laugh. I was quite chuffed that he was amused with one of my anecdotes.

Many times I had come up against different English gangs with Cardiff. Now all these boys, plus many more, were to descend on London and I couldn't wait to speak to as many as possible and spread the word about Cardiff. There was word of other Cardiff fans knocking about and Neil and Mark from Wrexham also turned up. They are just like me, they have to have their regular fix of football. I have known them for years from following Wales away and so on and they have become good mates but I couldn't resist bugging them about Wrexham getting chased by Cardiff in the Welsh Cup final. Neil hasn't heard the last of that but what happens on the day happens and we never let it become personal. Mind you, if Wrexham ever did the Soul Crew (on Fantasy Island maybe) then it might be different.

We moved to a different pub. The word was that the Hibs Capital City Service crew, Aberdeen and the rest of Scotland's main firm were up at High Barnet, North London. Rumour was that 300 of them were being kept in two pubs heavily guarded by police. I wanted to see some action so we caught the Tube to Wembley, even though we didn't have tickets. Walking up Wembley Way we saw a few scuffles but mainly between drunkards. Myself, Neil and Swaley, one of Tottenham's main lot, then thought we'd get a taxi back to Camden, as word was that a lot of lads were heading back there.

The game had just kicked off when we took a cab to the World's End, a large pub near Camden Tube station. As we passed the pub, this big blond lad came over to me. He was dressed fairly smartly in a Lactose check shirt.

"Where's ya lads?" he asked, in a broad Scottish accent.

I replied, "I'm Cardiff, not English, look..." as I pointed to my badge. I don't think he could see the badge, he was that pissed. I could have been Polish for all he knew. By way of being friendly, he punched me in the ear. The three of us walked away as he shouted to his mates emerging from the World's End. *Here we go*, I thought. There were at least 30 of them and they steamed at us throwing glasses and bottles.

I ran, swerving in and out of the Jocks. It was every man for himself. As I was chased down some market street I heard two different shouts behind me. One was, "You'll never do the Celtic," and the other was something to do with Dundee. I got away unscathed but was beginning to regret my trip.

Then something came over me and I thought, *I'm Cardiff, fuck running from these Scottish bastards, who do they think they are?* I made my way back, preparing to make sure they looked at the badge. As I strode past the World's End, expecting more bother, I saw Neil talking to them. He called me over. Neil knows everyone, including half of these Celtic. I just wanted to get away from there so we left. He said they had caught him and he was scrapping with four of them until one recognised him as they were booting him. I don't know where Steve's mate from Spurs went, as we never saw him again. I hope he's okay!

We went back to the Spread Eagle. One of the Wigan lads was slung out over an argument with some stewards. As more kept coming in, we told them about our little brush with the Scottish lads, and they left the pub fuming. After 15 minutes in some other pub, ten of us decided to go back to the Spread Eagle. We could see the pub was packed inside and out, full of older lads all holding bottles. There were over 100 nasty-looking geezers outside. Most of them spotted us as we wandered near them. The first couple walked quickly towards us.

"You facking Jocks?" said a broad Cockney accent. They all looked ready to rumble.

"No," one of the Wigan replied.

Then I recognised some of the faces – they were Millwall. "He's not a facking Jock,' said one. 'He's facking Cardiff and they're facking Wrexham"

A few burst out laughing. Some of these Millwall I had known for years and they came over to greet us. I was surprised to see the main Chelsea Headhunters were also there. The two firms had buried the hatchet for this big occasion. Minutes earlier they had bumped into our aggressive little Scottish posse and fought them back into the Underground. Bricky, one of Millwall's main characters, described how Chelsea and Millwall combined had destroyed the Scots. I wouldn't have liked to have been those Jocks, bumping into this mob. TC, Chelsea's main chap, had his collar felt for the incident. Apparently the police had a van parked outside his house for the duration of the tournament.

They were also 30 Wolves there, who Neil knew from years ago. I had heard about a couple of them and had a good chat with one. They were among the best casuals there all day. I had a few enquiries about my badge and a couple of

snide remarks but I thought, *so what?* This massive lad from
Arsenal, who is well-known everywhere, was telling Millwall
he had earlier seen a nasty mob of ICF at Whitechapel. It was
"follow the crowd" for me from then on as they all began to
make their way to the Tube. There was commotion all over
with people running about and I didn't have the first clue
what was going on. We boarded the Tube, where I got
chatting to some Derby Lunatic Fringe, who told me how
much they rated Cardiff.

As we changed trains, I could see the mob I was with was
200-plus. This was definitely the main English lot out that
day and they meant business. I felt envious – for me it would
have been a dream to take a mob of Cardiff or Wales up to
Wembley. We got off near the West End but this mob knew
what they were doing. They took the back streets, or "back
doubles" as they are called in London. I didn't ask anyone but
I think something was arranged. I followed as they roamed the
streets.

They were getting close to Trafalgar Square when some of
the lads at the front started screaming, "Here they fucking
are!" As they turned the corner all I saw was bottles, glasses
and chairs come flying through the air at them. I got up the
front to see what was going on. There must have been 100
Scottish piling out of a café bar. This was it. They just
steamed straight into each other. For a minute it was pure
mental and I couldn't believe it but the Jocks were actually
getting the upper hand. Within seconds, though, police came
out of nowhere and turned their truncheons wildly on both
gangs and forced the Scots – who I presumed to be Hibs –
back into the bar.

I sneaked off with a few people and headed for Trafalgar
Square. The gangs of lads there were unreal, all sizing-up
each other. We moved on to Leicester Square and outside the
Hippodrome stood 80-100 lads. In the middle, with a gash on
his head, was Paul Dodd, the "superstar" thug from Carlisle.

As far as I could tell this group comprised Carlisle, Oldham, Shrewsbury and Newcastle, who for many years had formed an alliance when it came to soccer violence. I phoned Neil to tell him to stay away from Leicester Square, as he and Shrewsbury's English Border Front have a bit of a history, to say the least. Quite a few of this number looked like they had been involved in action.

A couple of Millwall walked past. The atmosphere was tense. They all looked pissed off and no-one spoke. It looked like it was about to go off between these Northerners and the Cockneys. I was told later that Carlisle and Mr Superstar bumped into a Tottenham firm and paid the penalty. The police then started to nick this crew and everybody dispersed. Rumours flew. Forest were taking liberties at St John's Wood, was one of many.

At Trafalgar Square it was as boisterous as before. I couldn't see many Scottish casuals but the blokes in kilts were weeding in. I got in a phone box and phoned Aberfan Steve. "Listen to this," I said, as charge and counter-charge went on between hundreds of English and the police. I said a few more words and he told me to be careful. The police were getting their act together and as I left the phone box they ran past me chasing a load of English down the road. One copper suddenly stopped, turned and shouted in my direction: "Cardiff!" It was one of the coppers who had me for Fulham in 1993. He was Chelsea CID. I knew then I had outstayed my welcome and legged it a bit sharpish into a taxi. "Paddington, please driver."

At Paddington there was still lads everywhere. *Who am I going to bump into next?* I thought. I stood outside The Dickens with my whopper and fries when out of the Tube station came a huge wave of lads: there was over 150 and many of them looked like doormen, with Stone Island, Burberry shirts and bald heads aplenty. It was Middlesbrough, and it was clear to see that no-one would have messed with these anywhere that day. I'd had a couple of encounters with this lot and they are one of the most serious firms I have ever seen. I got to speak to some who said they had just given a firm of Leeds a beating.

The thing with the English mobs out that days was that before the game they were all quite happy to join up, but once they couldn't find any Jocks, all the old personal battles were remembered and sorted out. I went home after seeing the cream of England's mob, impressed but by no means overawed.

I AM MORE Cardiff than anyone but, as I say, if the opportunity arises I love to watch other teams in action. It is an expensive hobby, granted, but too addictive to stop. Just a couple of seasons ago one of United's top boys gave a national newspaper reporter an insight into it. Before a league game on a Thursday night at Old Trafford, both sides had been involved in a vicious running battle at Salford Quays. There were stabbings and one of United lot nearly died with his throat cut. Months later Liverpool were due at Old Trafford in the FA Cup. The planned revenge was reported in this paper. A carfull of us travelled up and were told where United were meeting: a pub in the heart of Salford. Outside stood around ten police vans. Nearby a Transit van was found with an assortment of weapons, including petrol bombs and machetes. I witnessed this mob march up to the ground, 500 at least Man U accompanied by the local plod. Liverpool turned up with close on 300 but the police were too well prepared, as they are at most big games. I have seen Liverpool involved in a few battles. I saw them run Sunderland's firm before the Cup final of 1992 and they also took care of Birmingham in an FA Cup replay.

ANOTHER JAUNT TO the North-west which is a particular favourite with all football fans is Blackpool, the lively seaside town. The number of fans who have passed through there over the years must be unbelievable and I have been with City many times. The first was in 1989. We were losing 1-0 late on and around 200 Cardiff decided to leave. A couple of my local mates and I followed. Most of them were the main crew and they made their way around to the home end. There were big orange doors and some of the boys booted them and they swung open. "Come on," one of the Docks lads screamed and everyone ran in. Waiting inside were police and stewards. I just managed to see it kicking off before Cardiff were forced back out by police horses and dogs.

After the game, four of us ended up drinking with Cardiff's older boys. It seems laughable now but Naf Naf clobber was very popular at the time. It soon kicked off in Yates's Wine Lodge with the bouncers but we had had enough and went to the Palace nightclub, close to Blackpool Tower. We were all trousered up, ready to go on the pull, but everyone in there was E'd up dancing to the Mondays, Carpets and the Stone Roses. It was my first taste of the Madchester thing and it stuck. We ended up dancing like amateur Bezzes by the end of the night. Music and culture-wise it was the start of the top era for me.

After the club we wandered back to the bus, which was due to leave around 1.30 from the Bloomfield car park, next to the football ground. The four of us indulged in a little singsong about Cardiff. From the distance, a large group of lads started shouting and charged towards us. We had to kick away because there was loads of them. I was much fitter then so I managed to get some distance. In a situation like this you didn't want to look back but it was tempting. We all got back to the bus safely and to this day none of us has a clue who that firm was. I know Blackpool on their day can get a mob together but it could have been anyone. Strange though that it had gone one o'clock in the morning and they just seemed to be hanging around.

In May 1990 we needed to win at Bury to avoid relegation and I ended up on the psycho Docks bus that was going to Blackpool after the game. Bristol Rovers were in Blackpool chasing the title, so a clash was probable. Our bus met up with more Cardiff at Manchester Piccadilly and over 100 then left for Bury. The police were clocking our every move. Over 2,000 Cardiff turned up but despite a gallant effort the team were relegated. We skirmished outside with the police but there was no Bury mob.

We got back to Manchester and the papers had news of Leeds rioting at Bournemouth. Our plan was to go clubbing, and once at the seaside our coach met up with some other Cardiff. Around 70 of us went on a tour around the town. Cardiff hate the Wurzzles (Bristol) and love the opportunity of mixing it with them. As we walked along the busy seafront near Central Pier, some likely-looking lads came past.

"You Bristol?" Darren from the Docks asked.

"No, Newport" one said.

"Even fucking better," Darren replied and hit him so hard that he was knocked off his feet. The other Newport were chased off. You always get many other mobs in Blackpool at the same time and these Newport must have been on a stag-do.

Legend from Cwmbran came over and said, "Rovers were in the Manchester pub. There must be three hundred of them." Fair enough. I didn't know what everyone else was thinking but I didn't like the sound of that. They've got some big bastards and it could be a bit too much for us to handle but the lads didn't give a toss. Their idea was not to attack the pub but to get down the nearest side street and let them know where we were. So we waited down this side road. People tooled themselves up with bricks from a skip as a couple of Cardiff went back into the pub to let them know. Everyone was psyching each other up: "We're Cardiff, it doesn't matter how many they got." I just wanted to get it over and done with so we could go clubbing.

The boys who had gone to the pub came back excited. "Get ready" one shouted, "They're coming now". We waited and waited, then a handful of lads approached.

"Hey lads," one of them said. "There's a load of fucking Taffies about, we're gonna kill them. You with us?"

"Nice one" one of our lads said and smashed a bottle right over his noggin. They sprinted off. I couldn't believe they had walked into the middle of everyone thinking we were somebody else. I could still see them running in the distance, about five minutes after the incident. We had waited long enough, so we headed towards the Manchester. We turned the corner in one of the back streets. Twenty lads walked towards us. No one asked who they were, we just got straight into them. About five stood while the rest fled through some slots arcade. The five were kicked all over the place. One was even made to sing, "We love you Cardiff, we do" – everyone stopped pounding him because they were laughing so much. They were Rovers, as their badges and accents revealed. The rest of the evening was fight after fight. At one point the police chased us through an arcade. I jumped straight onto a bandit and pretended I was a punter as all this commotion was going on behind me. I played the bandit as a copper stood right behind me looking about.

Blackpool no doubt has hundreds of similar stories. One weird trip came the season after. On the night before, 15 of us left from Aberdare: myself, Hopkins, Gary M, Jumbo, Steve and the rest, all crammed into the back of a Transit. Also with us was a mate who basically was caught between the devil and the deep blue sea for years – he followed Swansea but grew up in Aberdare and all his mates were Cardiff. He knew all of Swansea's boys well but most of them resented him for having friends such as myself, who were staunch Cardiff. He also took much grief off many Merthyr lads who were Cardiff nutters. He came to Blackpool for the trip and as soon as we parked up he was recognised by Merthyr. They said nothing at first but later it violently kicked off between our van and theirs. He shouldn't have been there but then again he was a mate and didn't really want to be left on his own, bored at home, while we were living it up in Blackpool. The Merthyr lot were crazy for him. It turned really ugly, with baseball bats used, but it was all forgotten about weeks later.

On another occasion, the Leicester Baby Squad were at Bolton and turned up in Blackpool when we were playing them. It was the Saturday after our cup game in Liege so hardly any of our proper lads went, but the boys weren't needed as some of the Baby Squad were steamed by most of our beer bellies, who at times are equally up for the row. Loads got nicked and jailed for their part in proceedings. Leicester I felt were an overrated firm but that's just my opinion.

My haziest trip up there involved two of us doing so many Es that we forgot where we were staying and ended up walking around town looking for the digs, freezing. I didn't bother with the game the day after. I was a little bit tired.

CHAPTER TWENTY-ONE

Bushwhackers

Millwall. The very name epitomizes English football hooligan culture. In recent times the Soul Crew have entered into a bit of a rivalry with the South Londoners, who have held the reputation of being among the most fearsome fans in Europe for many years. I had heard all the old tales secondhand but my first experience of them came in February 1991. Cardiff were at Halifax for a nothing fixture and five of us decided to go on the train with that old favourite, the family railcard. How many football fans used to blag their way around the country with those? What was it now, the oldest person pretended to be daddy and paid a third of the fare, £12 I think on that day, with the kids going for a pound each and splitting the difference. It was a decent scam but we were thrown off trains more often than not, as happened that day.

We got to Halifax by half-time and they still charged us £4 to get in, the full price. After seeing a rare away win we got the train back to Manchester Victoria and made our way over to Piccadilly. The five of us were extremely distinctive in our Stone Island coats. Up towards a taxi rank, I saw out of the corner of my eye a group of older men kick past us. There were about 15 of them. We slowed down and one of them turned to us and came over, arms apart.

"You fuckin' City?" he demanded.

I assumed he meant Man City. "No, we're Cardiff" I retorted.

They came around us, "We're Millwall, Were looking for the fucking Mancs. We can't find them nowhere." We were awed as soon as the word "Millwall" was said. They seemed to take on a whole new stature. They were all 30-plus and one look told us they weren't your average 15 lads on a typical away day. They were really friendly towards us, however, especially after we told them where we had been. They sympathised. "We've been there," they said. "Done all the shitty trips."

"It won't stop you doing them again, though," one added. He knew what he was talking about.

They took us in the station bar and bought us drinks. We swapped stories but we were more interested in hearing theirs than telling ours: great tales of epic clashes with the likes of West Ham and Chelsea. Only weeks earlier, 28 of them had run Newcastle all over Newcastle city centre, which they were genuinely thrilled with.

I got onto the subject of Cardiff. They had the greatest respect for us. Two of them were in their 40s and one asked, "How's Frankie and Peggy doing?" – two of our terrace legends from the 1970s. "We fucking love Cardiff. You lot have always been up for it when we meet home or away."

These were real lads. A lot of thugs might have had a pop at us but they were different. We enquired about their Stone Island and they put us in the picture about a little store in London at Russell Square that had the gear at bargain prices. It didn't take me long to visit this gold mine: racks of top of the range Ice jackets, camouflage, the ones that change colour in heat, for around £50 a go; I bought two first of all, a Stone Island denim for £30 and a couple of CP tee-shirts for a fiver each. This place was a treasure trove for a while but soon after they put the prices up to match the other stores around so it was back to paying huge amounts once more.

Millwall were vying for promotion to the old First Division and the blokes said they had Bristol City away at the end of

April. They didn't much like Bristol City and invited us over for a look, and myself, Steve Weazle and Greeny from Barry arranged to meet them. We said our goodbyes and the Cockneys set off, saying that they had arranged with the Cockney Reds (Man U) for a small welcome-back-to-London fight when they reached Euston. They were all excited about it. That's the thing with London, there are so many teams there every weekend that it is guaranteed to go off somewhere, be it a pub, train or Tube station.

On the day of the Bristol fixture, we arrived at Bristol Temple Meads at 10.30am to be met by three or four Millwall. They had been out on the piss around Bristol the night before and sported a couple of black eyes to show for it. A call came over the station tannoy for one of them from a lad called Bobby. I later found out Bobby was the top lad at Millwall and he let the others know the train from London was due in. It arrived at around 11am and off came around 80. These were the proper Bushwhackers: there was no-one my age and hardly anyone under 30. The dress code was immaculate, almost military: Stone Island coats, CP Company and Bonneville, with no exceptions. We were to get to know some of these men well over the years but just by looking at them you could tell they each had a story. The police let them walk, shadowing them. They obviously knew where they were going and a couple of them took us through who was there. It was fascinating. "That's Billy there, his father got killed by one of the Krays. And that's Frank, who's just done fifteen years for manslaughter. And that's Charlie who's just done twelve for armed robberies." It was an eye-opener for a teenager from the Valleys.

As we approached a busy shopping street, I heard, "Its up here on the right." The police started turning up in large numbers. Millwall walked past a pub called the Hen and Chicken. The doors burst open and about 20 Bristol shot out throwing bottles and glasses, before being pushed back in by police. Most Millwall just laughed. The Londoners were moved near the canal to a pub called The Orchid and the police left us. We listened to their stories avidly, the three of us cramped at the bar with the Londoners trying to get a drink. It was a couple of years before mobile phones were common and we heard that Bobby had paid a taxi driver to go and tell Bristol City where they were.

Soon after some shouts came up, "They're fucking here." They couldn't get out of the doors fast enough. I was getting crushed by these grown men foaming at the mouth, squeezing out ten at a time at the door, drinks flying everywhere. I got out onto the street and turned the corner. I couldn't believe it: there were at least 300 Bristol City charging down the road but these Millwall sprinted towards them. The Bristol at the front had baseball bats, cues and I saw two golf clubs. Some Millwall were lagging behind and Bobby stood in the middle with his back to Bristol, grabbing people and screaming, "Come on Millwall, keep it together." As soon as the front line of the Bristol got close you could see hesitancy in their eyes. They threw most of their weapons. One with a golf club started swinging it. The first Millwall lad faced him, dodged from side to side and then grabbed the club.

Their bottle went and every one of them turned, to a man. Between 300 and 400 Bristol were chased, kicked and punched by the 80 or so Millwall. It was a sight. Bristol City tried to stand a few times but their moment had gone. They soon fled out of sight and the Millwall started hugging and singing their "Let them come to the Den" ditty.

We started going a few times a season with them, if Cardiff had a free weekend or a lousy trip. Games I saw included Birmingham at home, when a big crew of Zulus were ambushed at London Bridge train station and some put in hospital. These were the top Millwall and to be honest they always looked after us, us being a hell of a lot younger than them. The things they get up to away from football is nobody's business and it's true that football lads around the country now have their fingers in many "pies".

Two of our new friends came to Swansea in the FA Cup and witnessed the destruction of our rivals. I discussed many times with the Soul Crew just how we would cope if we did come face-to-face with Millwall for the first time since 1986. The occasion duly arrived in November 1996 in the Autoglass trophy. When Millwall heard of the draw I received a phone call from one of their main lot saying they were getting a coach sorted and word soon spread that they were coming. A few days before the game, however, they told me that only a few were now coming, in a car, so I said I'd meet them for a drink with a few of the boys, no hassle.

They turned up in the Albert near the station, 11 of them. There were a lot of Docks, Ely and Valley lads out who don't usually turn out unless we play a club with a decent crew. At one stage there must have been 60 Cardiff in the pub and you could cut the atmosphere with a knife. It was awkward but in fairness to our lot they got up and left when they saw the Millwall didn't have the numbers and weren't really up for it. With only four or five Cardiff left in the pub, I retired to the toilet to powder my nose with one of the Cockneys. A minute later the toilet door was booted open and one of our lot started fighting with the Cockney. I was more concerned with the "charlie" getting scattered everywhere as they carried on their fight on the floor. While we'd been in the lavatory, one of the Millwall in the bar was seen to adjust his cosh and remove a can of CS gas from his pocket. This was seen as blatant provocation and the handful of Cardiff had given them a hefty beating. I couldn't do anything to intervene and it was Millwall's fault anyway.

Many Cardiff are friends with lads from different English clubs and dozens of lads have come on their own or in twos to visit us home and away. Some of our older lot never used to grasp how you can talk to other boys these days but I liked the fact that these lads got to see us in all our "glory" and would go back to wax lyrical about our firm. But the hardcore would take offence at larger numbers turning up, as in this instance, and especially when they first call a fight on, then decide against it. It did play on my mind that they had always looked after us yet I couldn't do anything to save them. Perhaps I didn't want to intervene because it was their fault for bringing weapons into the pub. We've got a few people with short fuses who don't take kindly to things like that.

We kept in touch after but it was never the same. A year later we drew them again, this time at the New Den in the second round of the Autoglass, to be played a few weeks before Christmas. The interest was astounding for such a meaningless fixture. We agreed to keep it quiet until the game then let Millwall know we were on our way up. We had five coaches booked full of lads but in the end could fill only three: two from Cardiff and one from the Rhondda. But it was a cracking 150: the Docks, Ely, Canton, Rhondda Valley, surrounding valleys, and 15 doormen from around South Wales for good measure, out on a Christmas jaunt.

We got to London at around 4.30pm. Millwall were continuously phoning the boys, "Where are ya?" and "What ya doing?" and "How many have you got?" Who cares how many – that question is a sign of weakness. They told us to go to the Elephant and Castle, which we did. Around 5.30 someone called them and told them where we were. "We're here. Three buses, not one copper. It's up to you." We had an immovable firm on Millwall's manor, as they would put it, and the adrenaline was pumping overtime. I knew their top lads: they would already be having an inquest. The older Millwall would take this affront personally.

Not many teams have caught Millwall off guard on the Old Kent Road. I walked outside the pub, which was called the Elephant and Castle. A car full of lads slowly came past and a shout of "Tony" came from the window. It was Gregor: he knows everyone in London and goes with Millwall now and again. He gets some bad press among some of the London boys but every time I have spoken to him he's been a sound enough feller. I can't judge a person by hearsay.

"Fuck me," he said. "I can't believe you've got a herd here." Millwall had 40, tops, he said, and weren't moving. Gregor is a bit vocal and had had an argument with some Millwall over us being there. They had told us where to be but hadn't realised we'd have such a big mob.

We couldn't wait any longer and all left. It was already 7pm and we couldn't be arsed walking to the ground, so Millwall were informed we were heading to London Bridge. There were no Bushwhackers there either, apart from a couple of spotters. The Tube ride was eerie but superb – there is no feeling like it, the rush of blood on a night like that. We got out at South Bermondsey Tube station, about half a mile from the New Den. It was dark apart from the few streetlamps that hadn't been smashed. We got to the bottom of the steps by the road and a row of police were waiting. In the distance under the bridge, some silhouetted figures began to move closer. We picked up the pace and the lads at the front suddenly rushed through the police lines. "Soul Crew, Soul Crew," was the haunting chant.

The police fought desperately to keep us and Millwall apart. They managed this until we got under the bridge and had to turn left toward the ground car park. By now there must have been 60 Londoners and they weren't just football lads. Some were youngsters and one, of no more than ten years of age, was screaming, "You fucking Welsh cunts." A few women come out of the flats opposite to throw stuff at us. The police struggled as some Millwall got into our escort, only to be met with flurries of punches. The Millwall were then batoned away. Bottles started flying past our heads. What a place.

Among the 200 Cardiff in the ground were hardly any

"normal" fans – they had been put off by the reputation of the place. We sang our hearts out the whole game. To us this was a fine "result" and although Millwall wanted our blood the older Bushwhackers, when they calmed down, would admit what a display it was from us.

In 1999 we were promoted back to Division Two and guess who came out first on the fixture list: Millwall at Ninian Park, a Saturday afternoon fixture on the opening day of the season. Were they crazy? It was obvious, even to the untrained eye, that the police would be pushed over the limit for this one. The Internet hooligan sites, the new age propaganda machines, were in full flow. Threats and counter-threats issued from the cyber warriors.

I arrived in town at 10.30am. A pub in Grangetown had been picked by our top lads and word soon spread. I was no longer there to fight but to observe: I nowadays have more important things in life like, amazingly, a decent, steady job for the first time since leaving school. I met two lads from Plymouth and a mate from Stoke and both were shocked to see how many we could raise. At 11am, 30 Millwall and a few of their QPR allies were escorted to Sam's Bar, at the edge of St Mary's Street on Mill Lane, the "continental quarter" of Cardiff. Three Cardiff lads went in and started straight away. Following this the pub was attacked by over 300 Cardiff. One of the Plymouth lads said, "This is the best crew I have ever seen." I told him that it was only half eleven and that he should wait until later.

The police swarmed town but found it near-impossible to stop the trouble due to sheer numbers. Around 12.30, another 150 Millwall arrived and were escorted to Sam's Bar. I saw all their faces. It was their best. Again, there weren't many under 30 and they had some right gruesome-looking bastards – but so did we. Cardiff met in Grangetown and decided to go around the back of town, down Penarth Road, to have a crack at the extremely well-policed Millwall. The crew that left was of gigantic proportions: 600 at least. No kids, 600 hardened lads, all the faces I had grown up with following City: Aberfan, Aberdare, Rhondda, Blackwood, Ely, Llanishen – everyone was there. The few English lads with us were now in disbelief.

As we approached the edge of town, two police on bikes drove past and radioed. One of them was dragged off his bike and thrown to the floor. A helicopter arrived and more police, who charged at us with their shields, only for Cardiff to stand and fight back. It was mayhem for a few minutes until horses and riot police finally put Cardiff back. It was a boiling hot day but the trouble was relentless. Millwall's escort was attacked all the way up Penarth Road to the ground and the police no doubt were glad to get them inside. At one stage a number of Cardiff got into the park in Grangetown just seconds away from Millwall, only for the helicopter to land between them, a most amazing sight at football match.

Missiles were thrown to and fro during the game (which ended with Millwall keeper Tony Warner getting charged with ABH). The game finished 1-1 but the best – or worst, depending on your viewpoint – was yet to come. This was another one of those days when, for whatever reason, the police lost the plot and let their guard down. Usually after the game, if the boys start congregating outside the Grange End the police can easily force everyone away. Today was different. There must have been 1,500 Cardiff waiting outside, not including the kids that went into the car park to throw stones and bottles. There is a video doing the rounds and the camera doesn't lie. Believe me, it was shoulder-to-shoulder, a sea of bodies, as a drain, among other things, was thrown back and forth over the Millwall end. You couldn't even pick your arms up at one stage, it was just a wave of Cardiff fans trying to force their way past the police towards the Grange End gates.

Suddenly the gates burst open and out came the first lot of Millwall. The police were helpless as they ran straight into Cardiff for a toe-to-toe battle for 30 seconds, until the sheer numbers forced them back in. I recognised some of these Millwall, game as anything, fair play to them. Things seemed to calm down but minutes later, astonishingly, the doors under the Grandstand burst open and about 40 Millwall came rushing out. Two of them had mops, I kid you not. They must have emptied the cleaners' cupboard on the way out.

These Millwall, although fearless, can't have known what was waiting for them. In all my time following Cardiff I couldn't have handpicked 50 worse people for them to bump into: I'm talking about some of the toughest men we have got. Millwall got savaged. Two were immediately knocked out, the rest chased back in. Some were caught as hundreds of Cardiff joined in. The beatings that Millwall took underneath the stand were vicious. Those running away got stuck under the stand as more Millwall tried to come out to join them. They were crushed under the stand and were helpless. All were given a hefty beating.

Enough was enough and eventually the Cardiff stepped back, leaving many Millwall injured in a big heap. It could have been even worse but fortunately the Cardiff there realised that Millwall couldn't take much more and I'm glad they quit before someone was seriously hurt. On the way out I even saw two Millwall men in their thirties crying on the floor. It was a fair fight, no weapons, no police, but it was too much for them to handle. Fourteen people were injured, with many needing hospital treatment. I have spoken to a couple of Millwall since and they have said they have never seen anything like it. Police dawn raids followed against many people, mainly youngsters caught throwing missiles. One lad was nicked for walking through town in the morning trying to get tickets for a rave at the ice rink. He had apparently never been to a game in his life but had seen the commotion and joined in.

The return game in December saw the biggest police operation ever for a league match in Britain. The authorities were not prepared to let it happen again and it didn't. Our normal fans didn't travel but still we had over 700 there in a frightening mob. We were herded all the way; they even shut down a couple of Tube lines just for us. Back at Victoria after the game was crazy, with Japanese tourists taking photos of us and people staring in disbelief as this army was brought through the station. Millwall rioted around the ground but to no avail. I don't think there was a punch thrown all day.

CHAPTER TWENTY-TWO

The Final Whistle

TO ROUND OFF the 1999-2000 season we had to go to Stoke City's new Britannia Stadium to get points to avoid relegation. There had been a small skirmish when Stoke came to us in the previous November. Twenty or so of them had bumped into a group of Cardiff at a city centre pub and been chased off. We had taken large mobs everywhere that season – Millwall, Wigan, Preston, Bristol City – and it was obvious the police would mount a major operation to prevent serious trouble at Stoke. We were well aware that over the past 15 years Stoke had been regarded as one of the leading mobs in England. As the saying goes, "They know we're coming and we know they're there." All week preceding the game the TV and Press warned of the biggest anti-hooligan operation ever in Staffordshire. They warned Cardiff fans that trouble would not be tolerated. As it happened, normal fans would suffer at the hands of over-zealous policing bordering on the ridiculous.

The boys arranged to meet in Stafford early and train it into the centre of Stoke, where they knew the locals would be. If they tried to get straight into Stoke they were sure the police would take them straight to the ground hours before kick-off – which is exactly what happened to most of the Cardiff fans. An irresistible force of around 350 got together and made their way from Stafford on the train. Again, I was along strictly as an observer: I knew it would come in handy for this book. But at Stoke station we were greeted with the usual police cameras in faces and yours truly had to endure a serious warning from a couple of the local spotters. I'm not stupid. A game that high-profile with cameras in every place rolling relentlessly was not the place for a known ex-face to make false moves. When you are young and not so well known you chance your arm.

Coaches were waiting outside for us to be herded in like cattle. Lots of pushing and shoving ensued as this huge crew tried to get on the buses. Already tensions were running high. Stoke police didn't help matters by drawing their truncheons at every opportunity. Lots of Cardiff failed to get on the buses and it became chaotic as police on horseback bullied their way through. Then it turned ugly. Windows on at least two coaches were getting kicked out, smashing on the road, and seats were hurled out at the police. The first driver then refused to go any further and we were told to get off the buses.

This is what the Soul Crew had wanted all along. They knew it would be treble on top with the law but still wanted to be able to walk it and get alongside Stoke's firm. The police plans were in tatters. They had to escort us on a dual carriageway to avoid the town centre. We saw a few Stoke but not too many. It was a long hot walk with loads of stoppages and we arrived just after kick-off. Cardiff were already 1-0 down. After frisking and more filming we were allowed to make our way in. Most of our lads went underneath the stand to have a pint.

The away seats were in two stands, one upper and one lower. The lower seats were left empty for segregation, with rows of tape in the way. This was little deterrent though and dozens of Cardiff forced their way down, ripping the tape. Soon after, hundreds of the boys were downstairs. Stoke had visible large groups of dressers to our left and right. We were told by one of our spotters that representatives from Forest and the Dundee Utility Firm were present. The atmosphere was extremely volatile, a powder-keg, and soon there was fighting with stewards and then the police. The riot police held it together enough in the ground to quell it.

The Bluebirds eventually lost 2-1 and we were subsequently relegated, again. After the game the inevitable happened. From the away end car park large fences had been erected to barricade us in. These were torn down and Cardiff charged up the banking towards the few hundred locals who were behind another large fence. Around 400 Cardiff surged towards them and tore at the final fence as more baton-wielding coppers stormed around on the offensive. Cardiff had to retreat down the banking. One fan got tangled up between some riot police and seemed to be getting attacked on the floor. This lit the fuse. The huge mob of Cardiff charged back and a pitched battle with the riot police ensued. They eventually had to turn and run and two officers ended up on the floor. In the coach park there were more fights with the police, who continually sprayed CS gas. The train mob were later escorted back with no real sign of Stoke.

Several months later it happened: over 100 Cardiff fans were arrested in "Operation Javelin." Raids all across South Wales took place based on video footage of events in and around the ground. There was even a nationwide photo campaign to locate 64 Cardiff, run continuously by the Welsh Press. What ever happened to innocent until proven guilty? Some friends of mine lost their jobs because of this and human rights went out of the window. Yes, some were found guilty and charged but others were found not guilty. Some collected prison terms and the majority of those convicted received bans of up to ten years.

Stoke police have clamped down heavily on their own fans of late and, fairly or unfairly, they thought it was time a few of our lot suffered too. Operation Javelin undoubtedly helped to curtail hooliganism at Cardiff for a while and some people thought it would stop it altogether. I suspect they are wrong. The events in the FA Cup at Leeds, described in the Foreword, suggest what could happen if Cardiff were to win promotion and to regularly play against bigger clubs. No doubt the police and football authorities breathed a huge sigh of relief when Tranmere Rovers knocked us out in the next round.

Reams have been written in the newspapers about that third-round FA Cup tie but most of it was gross exaggeration. Ninety-nine per cent of City fans were gutted that the media chose to concentrate on what was basically an exuberant pitch invasion rather than a famous defeat of one of the best sides in the country. What certainly was true, however, was that Cardiff that day had 1,500 boys out – the best mob at home since Manchester United in that now historic game in 1974 (which brings this book nicely full circle). Leeds were expected to come in force and there were claims on Internet chat sites that they would have their best mob out for years.

In the event, several hundred Leeds hooligans did rendez-vous at Hereford but they were well policed all the way into the city. A mob of 150 did arrive at the train station at about 2pm but the police blocked off all the approach roads to the station and beat back all attempts by Cardiff to reach them.

At the time of writing, Cardiff the city and Cardiff the football club are finally realising their potential. The state-of-the-art Millennium Stadium will be home to the FA's and Football League's major games for the next four years at least. The place is buzzing and with Sam Hammam's takeover of the Bluebirds in 2000 and with him ploughing millions into the club – culminating in instant promotion to the Second Division – the fans have regained some of the pride that went missing for years under penniless regimes and broken promises.

Hammam has upset people in the past and I am sure that a lot of the criticism over the Leeds game was the result of old scores being settled. He stuck his neck out and the Cardiff fans love him for it. What he has said about the Soul Crew is that he respects many of them because he has got to know

them and they are loyal supporters. Through a good friend
with connections to the boys, Sam took two coaches of our
finest for a champagne and lobster end-of-season reception at
a five-star hotel in Mansfield to celebrate promotion and say a
big thank you to the Soul Crew. He had got to know one or
two influential lads and they got in touch with the rest of us.
Many of the main faces were there. It is reckoned that up to
80 bottles of Moet champagne were consumed and Sam
spent about £8,000. He was really friendly and down to earth
and said he loves the warmth of the Welsh people. He was
later quoted in the *Sun* and the *Daily Mirror* as stating, "I was
proud to travel with the Soul Crew." Class.

Maybe those years in the doldrums explain why there has
been so much trouble. I am sure that if they followed a
successful club in the First Division or Premiership, the off-
field activities will be more limited for many. I have always
been as proud of my football club as anyone. For years the
ridiculous rugby-orientated media and outsiders have scoffed
at Cardiff City and our fortunes. Nowadays they are all taking
the club a little more seriously. Hopefully the proverbial
sleeping giant is waking. Ninian Park has been revamped,
with a roof back on the Grange End. Season tickets have hit
an all-time high and plans for a new stadium and our gateway
into Europe are under negotiation.

Maybe it's another false dawn but as our song goes, "I'll be
there." You hear about the corporate and hospitality moanings
of fans of the big clubs; personally I can't wait to be in one of
the executive boxes at City's new stadium watching us devour
Arsenal 4-0, drinking champagne but maybe not the prawn
sandwiches! Let the good times roll.

Both Dave and I will continue to count many of the Soul
Crew among our best friends. Only in the past few years have
I secured a good steady job and, now that I'm approaching
30, I have calmed down, mellowed and, in some people's
eyes, grown up. Dave Jones and I do not intend this in any

way as a "hooligan handbook" or an exhortation to go out and commit acts of violence. We just wanted to tell it like it was in those crazy days we both experienced following this special club of ours – Cardiff City AFC.

Cardiff City Honours

English F.A. Cup Winners	1927
English F.A. Cup runners-up	1925
English F.A. Cup semi-finalists	1921
F.A. Charity Shield Winners	1927
Division 1 runners-up	1924
Division 2 runners-up	1921, 1952, 1960
Division 3(south) Champions	1947
Division 3 Champions	1993
Division 3 runners-up	1976, 1983, 2001
Division 3 third place and promoted	1999
Division 4 runners-up	1988
Welsh F.A. Cup Winners	1912, 1920, 1922, 1923, 1927, 1928, 1930, 1956, 1959, 1964, 1965, 1967, 1968, 1969, 1970, 1971, 1973, 1974, 1976, 1988, 1992, 1993.
European Cup-Winner's Cup semi-finalists	1968

Tony's Acknowledgements

Many thanks in no order to Geraint, Gareth (still keeping it real) and Ceri, Paul (Flash), Jonesy, AA, M, Pugsy, Picky and the Mount Boys, Sarah T, Modgey and Suzanne, Chris P, Jumbo, Gary M and Lisa, Bunnsy and Dawn, Lyn S, Budgie, Steve Moog, Woody, Dion, Gethin, Rhys, Ryan H, Martin H, Jamesy, Bonzo, Marxy, Michael Doran, Andies, Kenny U, Peter J, Tony G, Sweedy, Simon Jones, Gary Pugh and all the Aberdare boys, Leon, Rory, Thommo, Lee Bryce, Kevin and Bianca, Adam, Vaughny and the rest, Stud, Dai and Donna, Kirsty, Ruth, Giggsy T, Ted, Hazy, Lee, Rob, Josh, Gary, Grant and the rest of the Aberfan class, Mark, Big Sam, Jaffa, Lyndsey and Rhiannon, Ceri B, Barwood and Bow, Shaun, Anthony Bevan and Kerry, Kirkby, Blond Simmo, Helen Thomas, Birmingham Steve, Rhys and Ange, Sherby, Beefy, Lizard, Newt and Kelly and the Rhondda SC men far too numerous to mention. Thanks also to Big Tec, Little Tec, Chris Price and the Ystryd Mynach SC, Neil, Chaz, Pearce, Will and Kev of the Wrexham Front Line, Chris of Caerphilly, Pete Lintern, Des, Parker, Christian, Craig B, Craig McGowan (for the patience), all the Gingers I know: Ginger Jones, Ginger Jason, Ginger of Taffs Well, Ginge LFC; Granville, Simon, Keith, Rhysy, Adie and the rest, Hurley, Jesse, Pricey, Gwillym Boore, Glenn V, Lug, Gonk, H (our own Alan Partridge), Willow, Gabby, Noddy, Weazle, Zeddy, Daniel and CC, Jacko and Jammo, Guppy, Eddies, Dai Virus,

Harding, Harvey, Jason Law, Ross, Quirky, Jonathan Owens and Conners of the Merthyr Massive, Nick and Dave (watch the Bluebirds fly), Alan Lewis, Marco, Jason E, Bobby, Rob, Kirwan, Jim, Hugh, Martin, Jocko, Johnny W, John, Faz, Romford, Kirkby, Mark and the Airdrie Boys, M Osti, Forrester, Midge, Mike, Bry Cannon, Duffy, Parr and the Wigan goon squad, Nick, Pasty, Chelsea Pat, Little Gregor, Paul from Reading, Piper NCFC, Scott from Carlisle, Mirko (Stoke City), Ryan (EBF), Dave, Tony, Mike, Walker (TCE), Gully, Woody, Bolton, Quinny, Nigel, Winkey, Simon, Mike and the Cwm lot, Richy Blackwood, Richy Bridgend, John, Gareth, Robbie, Brad, Richy, Karl and Ashley from Hereford, Prosser, Rosser (where's me trousers?) Richard and the Porth Dublin 2001 Party People (stay back, lay back!), Suggsy, Vampy, Ricky W, Wally, Colin, Cadge, Wilburs and the Roath men, Shane, Moggy, Julian ,Stanley and the Llanishen Posse, Sarah E, Shaun Smith, Sherbet, the family Simmonds, Neath, The Punk, Phyllis, Matty, Sandham, Scouse, Nigel, Gary J, AP of Port Talbot *aka* Tom Jones, Simon Williams, Clancy Wiggum, the Bishop Brothers, Sully, the Docks, the Brownhills Dirty 30, The VCs, the Doughnut Mob, the Barry Boys including Kirsey, Jurgey, Dibble, Darryl, Marshy and Jeff, everyone who contributed and anyone else who's a Bluebird through and through, Dai Thomas, Steve Coogan, Dan, Danny and the Liverpool Urchins, DJ, Darren of Penarth, Dai H, Dom from Torquay , D.Hapgood, Chris and Tommy Collins, Kippax, Gareth and Sam Hammam. To these friends who are sadly missed, Tom B, Paul B, Rory M, Paul J (RIP). Apologies to anybody I have forgotten. Last but not least, my family who have always been there no matter what. Love and regards.